Speaker's Handbook
of Successful
Openers and Closers

Also by the Author:

Handbook of Inspirational and Motivational Stories, Jokes and Anecdotes, Parker

Complete Speaker's Galaxy of Funny Stories, Jokes and Anecdotes, Parker

Pursuit of Happiness, Bethany

How to Stop Worrying—Forever, Pelican

505 Jokes you can Tell, Bethany

How to Make Money Speaking, Pelican

2121 Funny Stories and How to Tell Them, Bethany

How to Win Your Audience with Humor, Simon & Schuster

Speaker's Handbook of Successful Openers and Closers

WINSTON K. PENDLETON

Prentice-Hall, Inc. ● Englewood Cliffs, New Jersey

Prentice-Hall International, Inc., *London*
Prentice-Hall of Australia, Pty. Ltd., *Sydney*
Prentice-Hall of Canada, Inc., *Toronto*
Prentice-Hall of India Private Ltd., *New Delhi*
Prentice-Hall of Japan, Inc., *Tokyo*
Prentice-Hall of Southeast Asia Pte. Ltd., *Singapore*
Whitehall Books, Ltd., Wellington, *New Zealand*
Editora Prentice-Hall do Brasil Ltda., *Rio de Janeiro*

© 1984 *by*

Prentice-Hall, Inc.

Englewood Cliffs, New Jersey

Fourth Printing . . . . . March 1988

Library of Congress Cataloging in Publication Data

Pendleton, Winston K.
   Speaker's handbook of successful openers and closers.

   Includes indexes.
      1. Public speaking—Handbooks, manuals, etc.
2. American wit and humor.   3. Anecdotes.   I. Title.
II. Title: Openers and closers.
PN4193.I5P44   1984   808.5'1   84-9794
ISBN 0-13-824525-8
ISBN 0-13-824517-7 {PBK}

Printed in the United States of America

To my favorite author and dear friend,

Elizabeth Linington
Dell Shannon
Lesley Egan

INTRODUCTION

How This Handbook Can Help You Open Your Speech with Force and Power and Close It Effectively and Dramatically

This book explains why the opening and closing of your speech are so important. It tells why you must grab the attention of your audience during the first 30 seconds of your speech. And it shows you how to do it. It also illustrates how to bring the curtain down on your speech so that everyone will remember you and your message.

The Speaker's Handbook of Successful Openers and Closers has been written and organized with you, the speaker, in mind. It includes hundreds of openers and closers, both humorous and serious. It is filled with examples that you can use or that will stimulate you to write your own.

As a speaker myself, I know how important it is to be able to find quickly and easily an opener or closer that will fit a particular situation. Therefore, this *Speaker's Handbook* features three separate and distinct keys for finding exactly what you need at a moment's notice. The material is arranged by topical category with an extensive system of cross-reference plus a Double Thematic Index.

The Table of Contents immediately directs you to each of the 439 major categories, which are arranged in alphabetical order throughout the book. Once you have read and evaluated the material under the heading you've selected, you'll find right there, at your finger tips, the numbers of related stories located elsewhere in this handbook. You can then turn to this additional material, giving you an even greater selection from which to choose.

The third valuable key for finding the exact opener or closer that you need is the Double Thematic Index. Instead of one index that might refer you to an opener when you really are looking for a closer, each division has its own Thematic Index. This bonus feature gives you scores of additional listings for locating the dramatic story, anecdote or quotation that is perfect for your use. And it speeds up and simplifies your search.

But there's more here than that. The first chapter goes into the importance of your opening remarks, and discusses when and how to use humor and when to start on a serious note instead.

It gives suggestions for preparing a power-packed closing for your speech rather than let it dribble along to a slow, dull death.

One chapter shows you how to tailor specific openers and closers to fit a particular audience or situation or subject. It describes how to find one in the book and give it a "twist" that will make it uniquely yours.

Another chapter contains actual examples. Here you will find quotations from many of the top-ranked public speakers in America. This valuable section of the *Handbook*, "How The Experts Do It," required tireless research, and is itself worth the price of the book.

HOW TO USE THIS BOOK

A Working Example

Let us say you have been invited to deliver the graduation address at a high school. First, you would look in the "Openers" section under the heading "Graduation." There you will find several openers that will get the attention of your audience instantly. You will have a choice of a humorous approach or a serious beginning, depending on your own feelings.

After putting several of the ideas together, you might start your speech this way. "I want to begin by saying this: *(#189),* I'm here to speak to you who are graduating. Your parents and the other guests may listen if they like, but tonight I'll be talking to you, because you are the most important people in this auditorium."

That should take you about 12 seconds. If you say it loud enough and distinctly enough, you'll have those kids' attention. To hold it, and make them want to listen to the rest of your speech, you can tickle their interest with a bit of humor, or you can startle them with a dramatic and serious statement.

Let's try the serious follow-up first. You could say, *(#190)* "Yes, you are important because you are the people who will be running this town, this state, and this nation. Some of you will be the doctors, some the lawyers, and some of you will serve as our government officials." That second part took 16 seconds. So, within the first 28 seconds you have captured the attention of your listeners. You then move into the main body of your speech in which you inspire them to great things.

Before discussing how to end this speech, let's go back and try it with a humorous opening. You begin with the same 12-second opener and move directly to the humor, something like this: "I want to begin by saying I'm here to speak to you who are graduating. Your parents and the other guests may listen if they like, but tonight I'll be talking to you. I hope you will listen to what I have to say because I have been listening to you. Yes, I was listening to some of your chatter a while ago when I walked down the hallway where you were lining up to march into the auditorium. And I looked you over—and I listened. *(#188)* I saw one boy and girl standing there holding hands. A few feet away I heard one young lady whisper to her friend, 'Look at them. Don't you think they were made for each other?' And her friend said, 'I certainly do. She's a headache and he's a pill.' " Total time for that opening—46 seconds.

If you decide to go this route and make the kids laugh, then you will want to follow that one up by saying, "I heard one young man say to the fellow standing next to him *(#191)*, 'I'll bet you are glad to be graduating. Because you sure did hate school didn't you?' 'No,' his friend said, 'I didn't hate school, I just hated the principle of the thing.' "

So, you have a choice—humorous or serious.

Now, what about the ending?

If you want to follow up that serious opening, you might use it as your closing too. You would say it like this, "As I said at the beginning of my talk, you are the most important people in this auditorium because you are the people who will be running this town, this state, and this nation. Some of you will be the doctors, some the lawyers, and some of you will serve as our government officials. *(#575)* From this day on, please work harder than you ever have before. Please do your best. Please do your job well. Because the future is in your hands."

On the other hand, if you have kept the graduates in a laughing mood, you might want to end on a humorous note. If so, try this, *(#569)* "Before I finish my talk and sit down, I want to say one thing, and I want to say it loud and clear. I'm betting on you. And when I say I'm betting on the young people of America, I want the world to know I'm betting on a sure thing. And nothing is better than betting on a sure thing."

Then tell this story: *(#475)* "I had a friend who liked to bet on a sure thing. One day he went to the race track, and when it came time to put down his bet for the fifth race, there he was, standing in line with a wad of money in his hand. There was a rather wealthy-looking man standing in front of him. The man turned to my friend and said, 'How are you betting?' My friend said, 'I'm betting $1,000 on Blue Belle. I figure I've got a sure thing.' The other man said, 'That's not a sure thing. There are six horses in that race and Blue Belle is not the fastest horse. I ought to know, because I own Blue Belle.' My friend looked the man straight in the eye and said, 'I still think I've got a sure thing—because I own the other five.' "

And there you are. Either one of those closings will make those youngsters remember you for a long, long, time.

Good luck as you use the Openers and Closers in this Handbook to guarantee that your next speech will be a success.

Winston K. Pendleton

CONTENTS

"Where shall I begin, please
your Majesty?" he asked.
"Begin at the beginning," the
King said, very gravely, "and go on
till you come to the end: then stop."

—Lewis Carroll

"Alice's Adventures in Wonderland"

CHAPTER 1

Your Opening and Your Closing— The Most Important Moments

EVERY EXPERIENCED SPEAKER KNOWS that you must get the attention of your audience during the first few minutes of your speech or you'll be fighting an uphill battle all the way. They also know you must have a definite and positive ending if you want your listeners to remember what you said.

They all don't agree on exactly how to do it, but they do agree that the opening and the closing of your speech are the most critical moments when you're standing before your audience.

Robert Orben, one of America's leading humorists, speaking coaches and speakers says this, "An audience's first impression tends to be its last. We remember more of what is said earlier in a program than later. And so, you can't go wrong if you think of the first two minutes of your speech as an audition. It's a 120-second sample that has to convince your listeners that the remaining 20 minutes are worth their time and attention."

He believes that humor is the best attention grabber, and tells how he uses it himself. "I occasionally open with a series of self-deprecating one-liners when my introduction or my printed credits refer to me as an 'expert on humor.' With some amount of false modesty, I point out the correctness of that statement: *I am* an expert on humor. But before anyone gets too

15

carried away with that, maybe I'd better tell you the first thing I was an expert on—HOW TO PREVENT BALDNESS. (For many years I have sported a very short crewcut from which most of the crew has bailed out)."

He doesn't stop there. He follows that up with a couple of fast one-liners, "Immediately the bubble of self-importance bursts, but I try to make a comeback: 'Frankly, I never realized that I was bald until two weeks ago, when a fly landed on top of my head—and slid off.' Now for the final payoff and reverse spin: 'But I'm not really worried about it because I know there's a Biblical explanation for baldness. That's right—a Biblical explanation for baldness. It is written that the good Lord has created millions and millions and millions of heads—and those He's ashamed of, He covers with hair!' "*

Tom Hopkins, the nation's number-one sales trainer, reached that envied position because he takes his work seriously. He explains how he feels and what he does to get his audience's attention, "The main concept of a good speech can best be articulated by comparing it to a magnificent classical symphony composed and performed by one of the masters of music (Brahms, Mozart, Chopin). An eloquent performance on the platform strums the heartstrings of all the emotions and will be remembered and relived in the ear, eye and the mind of the audience.

"To achieve the above-mentioned emotions, I use a series of questions to immediately get the attention of my audience. For example, 'How many of you in this meeting are here with a desire to learn how to earn more money—raise your hands? I hate to disappoint you, but you will never learn how to earn money in a classroom—you will *hear how* but you will only *learn how* when you make yourself apply the techniques you will be hearing today.' "

Although, as he says, he knows the value of winning his audience in his opening remarks, he feels strongly that the closing of the speech is the most important part. "The majority of the people will remember most," he says, "that which they hear

---

*Reprinted with permission from *Orben's Current Comedy*, published by The Comedy Center, Wilmington, Delaware.

in the last 10 minutes of the speech. For this reason, it is critical a person write out, develop and structure a proved wrap-up that emotionally builds to a climactic experience with the end result of hopefully a standing ovation. However, after years of public speaking and over 1,500 presentations, I have come to the realization that if I do my very best and give the audience everything I have and don't receive a standing ovation, it is not my concern."

"Kirk" Kirkpatrick, award winning speaker and author of "Complete Speaker's and Toastmasters Desk Book,"* says bluntly, "The early part of your speech is the most important. The audience needs to hear clearly what you have to say. This is vital to gaining control of your audience. Whatever you do, speak carefully these first few moments as you spell out and magnify your theme to be sure the audience clearly understands what you are saying."

When Kirk talks to people about their speaking, he describes their introduction then says, "The time has come for you. The moment of truth. The point of no return . . . Now is the time for you to deliver. Never forget how important these first few moments are as you get started into your speech. The audience is already judging you and deciding whether you will be interesting or boring. Make everything count in your favor and you will have no problem gaining control."

He gives this succinct advice about ending your speech, "The close of your speech is terribly important. You can have such a memorable close that you will be remembered for some time by your audience."

"Close only once," he says. "All too often you hear speakers who reach several climaxes in their speech, leaving the audience to wonder when it is coming to an end and when the speech is over. Good material placed toward the end of a talk is highly important. Along with your voice, body language, and gestures, the speech can end dramatically and get the desired results."

Even though all professional speakers know the importance of those first few minutes, each has his own way of using

---

*Prentice-Hall, Inc., Englewood Cliffs, N.J., (1981)

them to get attention. Roger Masquelier, a homespun humorist from Mansfield, Ohio, tells how he approaches an audience, "My opening and closing probably would not fit anyone else, unless they had a personality like mine. It is easy for me to look confused and unorganized, as it reflects my mind. I start sentences that I never finish, appear to get myself in trouble with a thought, and for the first few minutes, am able to get so much sympathy from the folks in the audience who feel sorry for me that I could read the Preamble to the Constitution and be successful. By the time I'm into my talk, the audience is so relieved that things seem to be under way that they enjoy the relief. I never use funny stories either at the beginning, or at the end—always through the talk."

He uses the same sort of faltering approach as he nears the end of his talk. He explains it this way, "The close is about the same as the opening—I seem to be trying to find a way to stop, but try to summarize what I have been saying. But instead of completing every thought, I get the first part started, and let the audience come to each person's own conclusion."

Sometimes, the best way to get the attention of an audience is by shock. This is particularly effective when you want to stir a group into drastic action.

I heard a man do it one night at a PTA meeting. He used an old cliché as an opener, but it worked. He wanted to call attention to the drug problem among the junior high students. This is how he opened his talk: *(#77)* "Do you know where your kids are tonight?" Maybe he picked that one out of a book or off a bumper sticker. Who knows? But he made good use of it in that first minute of his talk. This is how he followed it up. "Oh you'll say, they're safe at home. Since it's Friday night and there isn't any school tomorrow, we said they could invite a couple of the neighbor kids in for cookies and cola. Right now, they're in our rec-room watching television? And you may be right. But what are they doing? Are they sipping on a can of beer that they sneaked out of the refrigerator? Or maybe a little of your innocent white wine instead of a cola? Or maybe one of those neighbor kids has brought along a few pills from his family's medicine cabinet and is daring your kids to try them. Please

don't misunderstand me. I'm not trying to scare you, but. . . ."
[Of course he was trying to scare them. And he did.] And from
then on, everyone in that room listened.

Another effective way to open or close an address is with
a quotation. You might open a Veteran's Day speech like
this: *(#253)*   "When Calvin Coolidge was president of the
United States, he said, 'The nation which forgets its defenders
will be itself forgotten.' Today, as we gather here, we come not
only to remember those who gave their lives for freedom, we
have come to honor them . . ."

The theme of a speech can sometimes be strengthened
and reinforced by using the same punch line to close it that you
used to open it. In a case of that kind, you might build your
entire speech around a quotation. Suppose you are invited to
speak on "Freedom of the Press." You could set the tone of your
talk with this famous quotation by President Franklin D.
Roosevelt. *(#316)*   "I want to speak today about a gift that
has been handed down to us as part of our American heritage—
freedom of the press. This is what President Franklin D.
Roosevelt said about this precious legacy, 'Freedom of conscience, of education, of speech, of assembly are among the very
fundamentals of a democracy and all of them would be nullified
should freedom of the press ever be successfully challenged.' I
come here to reaffirm what he said, and to point out how certain
despotic forces are trying to deprive us of this basic freedom . . ." You could use the same quotation to close your
speech. "I thank you for listening so attentively. You may not
remember much of what I have said because I am not a great
orator, but please think about those words of President
Roosevelt that I gave to you earlier; 'Freedom of conscience, of
education, of speech, of assembly are among the very fundamentals of democracy and all of them would be nullified should freedom of the press ever be successfully challenged.' "

James Arch, a speaker and teacher of speakers for more
than 30 years, feels strongly about those first few minutes of
your speech. He says, "The opening of a talk is very important.
It should not be left to chance. It should be carefully planned and
rehearsed and rehearsed. Getting your presentation off to a

good start is vital. Knowing you have a good opener will give you confidence and give time to settle down and make the audience feel comfortable.

"Never, never, never memorize your talk. The moment you forget something or get off track you are finished. However, by all means memorize your opening. Know exactly what you will say at the beginning . . . your first two or three sentences.

"And avoid these no-no's. Do not begin with an apology. Never begin by saying 'I am not prepared.' Who knows? You may fool them. If you are not prepared, the audience will discover it without your assistance. An apology is usually boring and no way to begin a talk and it is an insult to your audience."

He often opens a speech with a few humorous remarks, yet he warns the beginner of certain dangers of trying it. "Unless you are naturally funny," he says, "and have a tested and proved funny story which you know backwards, forwards and upside down and have the time and punch line off 'pat' do not attempt it. When you open with a joke and no one is laughing, it is very embarrassing and no way to start a presentation. It will shatter your confidence and make it extremely difficult to get back on track."

Which brings up the subject of humor.

Because I have earned my living as a humorous speaker for more than 30 years, I naturally lean toward the humorous opening. I find that it is a powerful card in the hand of any speaker who knows how to play it.

Some people think you must be born with a natural talent for humor. Having a "funny streak" or a natural feel for humor might help, but I think the skill of making people laugh can be learned.

The secret, if there is a secret, lies in how you tell your story. That is much more important than the story itself. There are hundreds of ways to put over a funny story. You might do it standing up or sitting down, you might be dressed as a clown or in a tuxedo. You might wave your arms and shout the punch line or you might stand quietly and with great dignity and whisper it.

Regardless of your particular story-telling technique, if you want people to laugh, you must follow two basic rules. First, you must know your story. Second, you must make it sound like the truth. It must seem plausible. Of course, there are several other elements involved in the delivery of funny stories, but if you don't understand the basics, you'll never be able to master the succeeding steps.

The first step in your preparation is learning to select the right story for the right occasion. Whether you are going to use it for an opener or a closer or to illustrate a point in the body of your speech, you must look for one that is funny—not merely clever. For example, puns are clever—sometimes extremely clever—but people rarely laugh at them.

So, be sure the story is funny. If you don't think it is funny yourself, don't dare put it in your speech. Maybe you heard another speaker tell it with hilarious results. You might have said to yourself, "That really wasn't very funny, but if he could tell it and make people laugh, I figure I can, too " Don't try it.

The moment you put a funny story in your speech it becomes your story. You are going to tell it. You must understand why it is funny. If you don't think it's funny, you can't convince your listeners. It's hard enough to get people to laugh at a story you really love and enjoy. So, don't flirt with the impossible.

Where do you find stories that people will laugh at? First, keep your ears—and eyes—open. They are all around you. You might hear another speaker tell a side-splitter. That's where your eyes come in. You not only hear the story, you can watch his body language as he tells it.

Your best source of funny stories is in humor reference books. There are dozens of them. The best books are those arranged by category and subject and cross-referenced. You can find them at your public library but better yet, you should have one or two of your own—within easy reach.

When you are deciding which particular story to tell, ask yourself what people laugh at. What's funny? You will find that people laugh at other people. They don't laugh at people who are genuinely suffering or in misery. But, they do laugh at people who have got themselves into embarrassing situations or predicaments because of their own stupidity or gullibility or conceit or greed or overeagerness.

Your audience will laugh at smart alecks and pompous and conceited individuals who get their comeuppance. And the person they enjoy laughing at the most is the story teller himself. Jack Benny was the perfect example. He was one of the world's great story tellers. When you laughed at him you were laughing at the always-trying-to-be-clever person who never succeeded—who always seemed to fall on his face.

So, whom will your audience laugh at? The obvious person is you. They come to hear you speak. They come to hear you tell about your experiences, your expertise. They are hoping they can relate to you as a human being. They are hoping you will not be talking down to them from an ivory tower. So, when you make yourself the butt of a funny story or two, they laugh at you—and take you into their hearts.

Rule number one then, if you are going to open with humor, is to tell a few stories on yourself. And remember this. They do not have to be true. They just have to sound true. And they must be funny.

You do not have to tell all of your stories on yourself. If you are a member of the community where you are speaking, you can kid and josh people who are prominent and in the audience. You might "pick on" the mayor and the president of the organization to which you are speaking. Or you might even poke fun at the organization itself. For example, suppose you are speaking to the local chapter of CPA's. You might say, "I don't know why I was invited to speak to you tonight because I don't know any more about filling out an income tax form than you do."

There is more to telling funny stories than that, of course, but if you will follow those simple suggestions, you will be on the right road.

Now we come back to that first question, "Why open or close your speech with humor? What use is it? What does it do for the audience? What does it do for you?"

First, let's look at the opening. I can think of five things that humor does for me during those first few minutes that I'm standing before my audience.

Attracts attention. There are occasions when an audience is handed to you in perfect order, that is, with absolute quiet in the room and with everyone giving you their full attention. On the other hand, you sometimes find that some members of the audience are whispering or chatting and not quite ready to settle down and listen. They might still be eating their dessert or lighting a cigarette. You might even be introduced (it sometimes happens) while some of the waitresses are still clearing off the tables.

In a situation like that, nothing will capture their attention as quickly as a funny story. If 10 percent of your audience are not paying attention, and suddenly the other 90 percent start laughing, you'll have the attention of that 10 percent by the time the first wave of laughter dies down.

Creates expectancy. Once you have won the attention of your audience with a wave of laughter, you will discover your funny story has gained you a second advantage. It has produced an air of anticipation throughout the room. Everyone is waiting for you to do it again. They expect to hear something worth listening to. They are eager to hear what you are going to say next.

Builds rapport. Once you have helped your audience laugh a time or two or even three, you will discover that something else has happened. They have become warmer and more amiable toward you. You have accomplished one of the most difficult tasks for a speaker. Within the first two or three minutes, you have established a perfect rapport with them. You have become friends. They feel as though they know you. They are glad you are there.

Relaxes your audience. When a friend drops by your home for a visit, you do everything you can to make him feel relaxed and comfortable. In the wintertime you might seat him in your most comfortable chair before the fire and offer something warm to drink. In the summer you might suggest that he take off his coat and tie and have something cool to drink. All of those acts are designed to make him feel at ease and contented. When you build rapport with your audience, you also are helping them relax.

Conditions yourself. While you have been attracting the attention of your audience and helping them to feel relaxed and in the proper frame of mind, something has been happening to you. You may not be aware of it, but in the process of making your listeners comfortable, you have been giving yourself the same sort of treatment. Nothing is more stimulating for a speaker than to hear his audience roar with laughter. When this occurs, you will find that you too are relaxed—your tensions and nervousness have disappeared.

Now you are ready to move into the main part of your speech, with you and your audience perfectly attuned to each other.

But what about your closing? How can humor help? What can it do to help end a speech?

Some speakers find it difficult to end their talk with a sense of finality. Many times they hem and haw, and murmur several "thank you's" or "good-byes," and generally end in an awkward manner. That's where humor can come to the rescue. It can play two important roles as you wind up your speech.

Help you end dramatically. Few words are as final or as conclusive as the punch line to a funny story. Once the punch line has been delivered, there is nothing more to say. Nothing needs to be said. The dramatic statement has been made and the roar of laughter takes over.

If you end your speech by sliding gracefully into an appropriate funny story, the audience will applaud and laugh at the same time. And there isn't a better sound in the world than that.

Make your audience remember you. If everyone who hears you will leave the room with a smile on his face and a laugh in his heart, you will be remembered. Some of them might even remember what you said.

And what speaker can ask for more?

CHAPTER 2

Make Your Openers and Closers Fit

CAPTIVATING AN AUDIENCE IS NOT DIF-
FICULT if you will study your audience, select appropriate
material, then tailor it to fit the group you're going to address.

Your opening and closing words must be relevant to your
speech or else they won't grip your audience at the beginning
and lead to a standing ovation at the end.

Your remarks are more or less like a suit of clothes. You
might pay a lot of money for a suit made of top-quality material,
but you would look odd wearing it if it were made for a 300-
pound six-footer and if you were only five feet tall and weighed
130 pounds.

The rule here is plain. You must tell the right story at
the right place, at the right time and for the right purpose. Like
a suit of clothes, your material must be tailored to fit the occasion.

Let me illustrate what I mean with a few examples.

You might be making a 20-minute talk to a men's
luncheon club. You decide to open with a bit of humor. You look
in the book and run across (#219).   It reads like this: "There
is a service club in Spokane where they grade their speakers. A
standing ovation rates four bells; an excellent speech wins three
bells; an average speech will give you two bells. If you make a

poor speech, you get one bell. They had one speaker who was awarded the no-bell prize."

If you opened your speech by giving that story word for word, you would look like the man wearing the baggy suit.

This is one way you could make it fit your own situation. "Thank you for that warm welcome. I hope you feel that enthusiastic when my speech is over. There is one organization that I know about where they grade their speakers. Each week in their bulletin they rate the person who spoke to them the week before. They put little Christmas bells by your name. If you receive a standing ovation, then you win four bells. If you are above the average, you get three bells. If you are average, you get two bells. If you do a poor job, you get only one bell. I spoke to them several months ago, and they awarded me the no-bell prize."

Suppose you are speaking in the high school auditorium to the annual meeting of a small town Chamber of Commerce, and you decide to open with *(#217)*. You find it in the book written this way: "A Baltimore newspaperman was speaking before a group of cattle ranchers in a small Texas town. He was almost frightened to death when he noticed that most of the men in the audience were wearing six-shooters. His fears increased after he had finished speaking and sat down, because one of the men drew his guns and rushed toward the head table. "Don't be afraid of him," the chairman of the group said, "He's not going to bother you. He's after the man who introduced you."

How would you make that one fit your situation? To begin with, nobody there wants to hear what happened to a newspaperman from Baltimore. They came to hear you. They want to know about your experiences.

So, alter that story to fit you. You might say it this way, "Several weeks ago, I was invited to speak to a group of cattle ranchers in Fort Stockton, Texas. Of course, cattle ranchers in Texas are cowboys. They held their meeting in a school house, just as you are meeting in here tonight. As that auditorium began to fill up with cowboys and their wives, I realized that most of those men were wearing pistols. That's something that will worry a speaker, but after I had been introduced I felt pretty good because the program chairman had said some nice things about me.

"Then, after I had spoken for about ten minutes, a great big fellow in the back stood up. He was wearing two guns and he pulled them out and pointed them at the stage where I was speaking. I want you to know I was scared. I stopped in the middle of a sentence and said to the chairman who was seated at the head table, 'What in the world is that fellow mad about? What's he getting ready to do?'

"And the chairman said, 'Oh, don't worry about him. He isn't going to hurt you. But, I sure do pity the man who introduced you.'" That then, becomes your story. And you have made it fit your situation.

If you are looking for a closer instead of an opener, you could use that same story. You might lead into it this way, "Before I close, I want to thank you for being such an attentive and courteous audience. I'm glad my speech didn't turn out like one where I spoke not long ago in Texas . . ."

When you call on your imagination and ingenuity, you can adapt almost any story to your needs. A story with the right message or punch line can be reworked to suit many different occasions. I have a friend who is particularly good at that. I've heard him on three occasions, and each time he told the same old story. But, he twisted it around to make it have a different meaning. The first time I heard him tell it, he was giving what is called a "classification talk" at his luncheon service club. This is the way he told the story: *(#211)*

"The other day my twelve-year-old daughter went to the public library and said to the librarian, 'I want to learn something about the Seminole Indians for my school homework. I wonder if you can help me.'

"The librarian said she would be glad to help her. 'You just sit over there at that table and I'll find what you want.' In about 15 minutes the librarian brought her a stack of books about two feet high and said, 'There you are. That will tell you a lot about the Seminole Indians.'

"My daughter looked at those books and said, 'Thank you, but I didn't want to know that much about them.'

"Now, I have been invited to give you a classification talk and tell you about my business. I am sure all of you are like my little girl—you don't want to know too much about it. So, I'm going to give you a five-minute look at what I do for a living . . ."

Some weeks later I was attending a PTA meeting where I had been invited to speak. A brief business meeting was to be held before I was introduced. As so often happens, a controversial subject had come up and it was being talked to death. After about half an hour of wrangling, my friend stood up. When the chairman recognized him, he told that same story and then said, ". . . I think all of us have heard all we want to know about the subject. I would like to vote on it so that we can get on with the rest of the meeting. I call for the question." And it worked. It worked because he made his story fit the time, the place—and his purpose.

As near as I can recall, I heard him tell that same story next at a neighborhood citizens' association meeting. It was obvious that a small clique was attempting to push through a resolution without allowing a full discussion of the subject. My friend stood up and told that story about his little girl and then said something like this, "I'm like my daughter. I don't want to know all there is to know about the subject, but I certainly do want to know more about it than I have heard thus far. I am sure there are others here who feel the same way I do. I have a couple of questions . . ."

I thought I had heard the end of that story until about a year later when he was the keynote speaker at a state convention of a trade association to which he belonged. His topic centered on a matter of legislation under discussion. He opened his speech with that old story about his little girl. Then he said, "Too many people today are like my daughter. They want to know as little as they can in order to get by in this world. I am glad you are not like that, and that you have invited me to explain in detail . . ."

I'm looking forward to hearing him speak again one of these days.

When you are putting a story or illustration into your speech, whether it is an opener or a closer or whether it is in the middle, be sure it is timely. Remember, some of the people in your audience might not have been alive when President Roosevelt and Prime Minister Churchill were in office. All they know about those two famous gentlemen are the facts they have read in history books. So, if you should run across a story about them in some reference book, change it around before you use it. Bring it up to date and make it fit your situation by telling it about two contemporary political leaders.

EXAMPLES FOR SPECIFIC OCCASIONS

The need to spend more money. You might be the chairman of a finance committee and must explain why certain proposals are going to require more money. You can prepare your audience for the bad news by telling them: *(#261)* "A fellow who lives in our neighborhood came home the other evening and found his wife crying. Having been married to her for more than 30 years, he was wise enough not to say anything to her. After he had taken off his hat and coat and mixed himself a drink and settled down in his chair to read the paper, she said to him, 'You don't love me anymore. You come home and find me crying and you don't even ask me what's the matter.' He looked up at her and said, 'I'm sorry, honey, but every time I ask you what's the matter, the answer ends up costing me money.' And I'm afraid that's the situation facing us. Our committee met, and asked the same question, 'What's the matter?' And I'm sorry to say that if we face the problem and answer it properly, it's going to cost us some money."

Individual accomplishment. This time the subject of your address concerns the importance of the individual—what one person can accomplish. You might cite two or three examples of such people as Thomas Jefferson, Susan B. Anthony, and Albert Schweitzer. You can close by giving a great rule for individual accomplishment that they can follow: *(#608)*

> I am only one. But I am one.
> I cannot do everything,
>   but I can do something.
> And by the grace of God,
>   what I can do—I will do.

Things are not as bad as they seem. If you want to deliver an optimistic talk in the face of a lot of dire rumors, try this approach. *(#204)* "We had a neighbor once who was a hypochondriac. She had been pestering all of the doctors in town for years. Nobody could please her. Then one day a new doctor moved to town. He had just graduated from medical school, and she was one of his first patients. 'I have heart trouble,' she told him. Then she spent about half an hour telling him about all of her symptoms. Finally she said, 'I do have heart trouble, don't I?' The young doctor said, 'No, not necessarily. With the symptoms you have described to me, you may not have anything seriously wrong with you. It might not be anything more than gas on your stomach, and that should be easy to cure.' When he told her that, she jumped out of her chair and said, 'Huh, you're nothing but a smart young whippersnapper. Why, you're just out of school. You have a lot of nerve, disagreeing with an experienced invalid like me.' I'm sure we have a great many members in our association who think our situation is worse than it really is. I would like to . . ."

Facing up to a problem. If you want to be serious from the first words you utter, try this bit of verse: *(#50)* "Something like two hundred and fifty years ago, a poet by the name of Aaron Hill said this:

> 'Tender-handed stroke a nettle,
>   And it stings you for your pains;
> Grasp it like a man of mettle,
>   And it soft as silk remains.'

"Today, our organization is faced with a rather thorny and nettle-like problem and I think we should face up to it and grasp it like men of mettle. I have a couple of suggestions . . ."

If you want to make the same speech, but want to open it

with a bit of humor, do it this way: *(#408)* "I had a friend who went to see his doctor. He said to him, 'I want you to give me a thorough examination and then tell me in plain words what's the matter with me. I don't want any of those fancy medical terms. Just tell me in plain language.' The doctor gave him a complete physical and then told him what he had found out. 'There's nothing wrong with you,' he said. 'And you asked for my diagnosis in simple language. This is it. You're lazy. Just plain lazy.' My friend looked at the doctor and said, 'Now, if you don't mind, would you please give the fancy medical term for it so I can tell my wife.' We are here tonight to talk about a problem within our great organization. I think we should quit kidding ourselves and admit we have a problem, then face it squarely and openly. I have a few thoughts on how to do that . . ."

Wise spending. If you want to make the point that bargain buying or purchasing from the low bidder is not always economical, you can make your point in the first minute of your speech with this bit of humor. *(#48)* "I was chatting with a friend the other day and I mentioned that my son's seventeenth birthday was coming up. If I bought him what he had asked for, I was going to be out two hundred dollars. And my friend said, 'Well, that's one thing you can say for my boy. He was seventeen years old three months ago and the gift he asked for cost me only seventy-five cents.' I couldn't understand how my friend could get off that easily, so I said, 'What in the world could you buy today for only seventy-five cents that would satisfy any normal seventeen-year-old boy?' 'Oh,' he said, 'that was easy. I gave him his own set of keys to the car.' Let's not be like that man. Let's not fool ourselves. When we begin to consider our budget for this year, let's look . . ."

Motivating your audience to act. When you are presenting a plan that you want your listeners to follow, you can make your point at the beginning of your speech with this story: *(#147)* "I had an uncle who did a bit of farming to supplement the pension he was getting from his old railroad job. His crops weren't flourishing, and the County Agent had dropped by to help him and to give him some constructive ideas. 'Turnips are going to bring a good price this year, and you have some mighty good turnip land. What do you think of that?' My uncle said, 'Oh, that sounds like a good idea, all right, but even if I get the seed, my old woman's too blamed lazy to do the plowing and planting.' And I hate to say it to this room full of friends and fellow members, but that's the trouble with a lot of us. We complain because the other fellow is too lazy to do our work for us. You can close with this one. *(#606)* Remember, there are no limits to what we can do if we work together except the limits to our own imagination and our determination to get the job done."

Recognizing an opportunity. When you are trying to put over a new idea, you can point out the importance of being alert to any opportunity that comes your way. Make your point at the beginning with this story: *(#281)* "When I was a boy we lived in a small tourist town in Florida. During the winter when we went to church, half of the congregation were visitors and strangers. I'll never forget one Sunday. Our minister preached only five minutes. When he finished his sermon he explained why. 'I'm sorry to cut my sermon so short this morning,' he said, 'but while I was eating breakfast our dog came into my study and chewed up my sermon notes and left me with only one page.' After church was over and the people were shaking hands with the minister, one of the out-of-town visitors said to him, 'I was just wondering if that dog of yours has any pups. I'd like to buy one from you and take it back home with me and give it to our minister.' There was a man who knew an opportunity when he saw one."

Or if you want to open on a serious note, say something like this. "Our organization is faced with a unique opportunity and I want to explain what it is and how we can make the most of it. But, in case my suggestions sound a bit ambitious, I want to remind you of what Walter P. Chrysler said one time. *(#282)* 'The reason so many people never get anywhere in life is because when opportunity knocks, they are out in the back yard looking for four-leaf clovers.' I hear opportunity knocking and I want us to open the door and let it in. . . ."

You might want to close with a humorous story. This one will make them remember that you urged them to grasp an opportunity. *(#667)* "Two friends were chatting. 'How are you and that new girlfriend getting along—the one you wanted to marry? Did you propose to her yet?'

'Yes, but she turned me down,' the other fellow said.

'What? Turned you down?' his friend said. 'You didn't impress her enough. Why didn't you tell her about your 90-year-old millionaire uncle?'

'I did,' the other fellow said. 'Now she's my new rich aunt.' "

Promoting a new idea. You may be called on to present a totally new idea to a group. You can impress them with the importance of solving old problems with new methods by opening with this bit of humor. *(#273)* "My neighbor has a little eight-year-old girl. The other day she brought home her report card from school. She had several A's and a couple of B's. A fine report card, but the teacher had written across the bottom, 'Betty is a smart little girl. She has only one fault. She talks too much in school. I have a system I am going to try, which I think may break her of the habit.' My friend signed the report card for Betty and then wrote just below the teacher's note. 'Please let me know if your system works on Betty because I would like to try it out on her mother.' "

Addressing a problem head on. You may want to jump into your topic feet first, without a lot of fanfare. Try it this way. *(#346)* "Last Saturday afternoon when the kids were playing in the back yard, I overheard my little boy talking to his friend from next door. They didn't know I heard them. I had just given my son a puppy, and his friend was complaining to him because his folks wouldn't allow him to have a dog. 'I've begged and begged and they always say no,' he said. And my little boy said to him, 'You just don't go about it right. You keep asking for a puppy. The best way to get a puppy is to beg for a baby brother—and they'll settle for a puppy every time.' My son got that idea from his mother. He sure didn't get it from me. Because I never beat around the bush. I speak my mind. And that's what I'm going to do right now . . ."

Maybe, when you talk about meeting a problem head-on,
you will want to do it yourself, with your opening words. See
how this fits your purpose. "I did not come here to beat around
the bush or to pussy-foot or give you a lot of sugar-coated
rhetoric. I came to talk about our problem directly and to urge
you to take a bold approach to solving it. I am reminded of what
Samuel Butler said one time: *(#158)* "If people would dare to
speak to one another unreservedly, there would be a good deal
less sorrow in the world a hundred years hence."

After that start, and with a powerful message about taking a bold look at whatever problem you are urging them to
solve, you could wind up with this serious punch line.
(#51) "There is an old Japanese proverb that says, 'Unless
you enter the tiger's den you cannot take the cubs.' "

The difficulty of communicating. You may want to
point out that communication, even within a group with similar
aims, often is difficult. Again, you might want to start with a
humorous illustration like this one: *(#91)* "Last year our
local church installed a set of electronic chimes, the kind that
work from a tape and with speakers that have adjustable volume
control. Our plan was to mount the speakers in the tower of the
church and play sacred music every Sunday afternoon. To make
sure that we were not playing them too loud for the people who
lived in the neighborhood, we sent out several teams of church
members to check on the volume level during our first concert.
One of our deacons rang a doorbell, and the lady of the house
came to the door. Our man said, 'I'm here from the . . .' 'What
did you say?' the woman asked. Our man said, 'I said I am here
from the church . . .' 'What did you say?' the lady asked again.
Our man now began to shout, 'I said I am here from the church
to ask you . . .' And the lady shouted back at him, 'You'll have to
talk louder, I can't hear a word you're saying on account of those
darn chimes.' If we are going to communicate so that we can
understand each other, we'll not only have to talk loud enough to
be heard, we'll have to get rid of the extraneous noise, and talk
quietly about our problems . . ."

Avoid acting prematurely. You may be called on to
speak against a proposal that you think requires more delibera-

tion. You can start with a funny story and end on a serious note. You might try this: *(#287)* "A man went to see his lawyer and said to him, 'I want to get a divorce. My wife hasn't spoken to me for three months.' The lawyer said to him, 'If I were you, I'd think about that for a while. Don't be too hasty. Wives like that are mighty hard to find these days.' I think we should postpone any action on this matter until after more of us have had time to study it and think about it."

Then, when you come to the end of your speech you may want to close it with a serious clincher, maybe like this: *(#676)* "Before I sit down, I want to urge you not to act too hastily. More than 2,000 years ago, the Greek philosopher Epictetus was speaking to a group of people who were faced with a similar decision. He explained it better than I can. This is what he said: 'No great thing is created suddenly, any more than a bunch of grapes or a fig. If you tell me that you desire a fig, I answer you that there must be time. Let it first blossom, then bear fruit, then ripen.' I suggest we follow his advice."

On making yourself understood. There might be a time when you are asked to speak on your particular specialty to an audience that is not familiar with the subject. You will be running the risk of becoming too technical or talking over their heads. Usually a bit of humor will clear the way for better understanding. You could say something like this, "Sometimes we get so involved in our own work and our own specialty that we assume other people know more about it than they do. *(#412)* Several weeks ago our little grandson was visiting us. When we went to Sunday School, we put him in the class with the other five-year-olds. His teacher opened the lesson by saying, 'Today we are going to study about Peter. Can anybody tell me who Peter was?' My little grandson raised his hand and the teacher said, 'Oh, this is nice. Our new little friend knows. Will you please stand up and tell all the other children—who was Peter?' And my little grandson said rather proudly, 'I fink he was a wabbit.' Now there was a kid who was trying to understand, but that teacher was talking about something else. So, if I begin to talk about things that you don't understand, please don't hesitate to interrupt me with a question."

To be cool-headed and calm. You may be called on to preside at an emergency meeting of some kind where people are wrought-up and angry. You could face your problem seriously from the start and open with something like this: "One time, more than 2,000 years ago, Aristotle was called on to preside at a meeting similar to this one. I'm going to open this meeting exactly as he did. *(#20)* This is what he said, 'Anybody can become angry—that is easy; but to be angry with the right person, and to the right degree, and at the right time, and for the right purpose, and in the right way—that is not within everybody's power and is not easy . . .' Maybe some of you have a right to be angry. But as we begin our deliberations, let us try to behave calmly and without malice or hostility."

The old pat-on-the-back. You might be called on to give an annual report in which you want to give credit to others. For example, you might be the outgoing president of the Chamber of Commerce and you want to commend your board of directors. Nothing goes over better in a case of that kind than a humorous opening. This would get you off to a good start: *(#81)* "A fellow back home one time bought a bottle of whiskey that was on sale. It was about the cheapest whiskey he could find. The next week when his yard man came to mow his lawn, he gave it to him for Christmas. Two weeks later when the man came to mow the lawn, he said, 'I sure do want to thank you for that liquor. It was exactly right.' The man who had given him the whiskey said, 'What do you mean it was exactly right?' 'Oh,' the lawn man said, 'If it had been any better you wouldn't have given it to me and if it had been any worse, I couldn't have drunk it.' And I want everybody here to know that the work that my board of directors did this year was 'exactly right.' "

A modest way to brag. Maybe you want to give a glowing report about the work that the members of your organization did during the past year on some special project. Start with this laugh-getter: *(#58)* "The other afternoon some of the neighborhood children were playing with my grandson in our recreation room. You know how kids are. They were bragging about how tough they were. One little boy said, 'I'm so tough that I can wear out a pair of shoes in six weeks.' Another one said, 'That's nothing. I'm so tough that I can wear out a pair of dungarees in six days.' But the little girl from next door had the best one. She said, 'You all aren't so tough. I'm really tough. I'm so tough that I can wear out my grandmother in six minutes.' Now, ladies and gentlemen, I don't want to sound as though I'm bragging, but I want to tell you about . . ."

Explaining changes or details. This opening will get you off to a good start when you are asked to explain the proposed changes in your organization's by-laws. *(#324)* "A young fellow called on me not long ago and said he was collecting donations for the local Boys' Club. I gave him ten dollars, and he proceded to fill in a card for me. 'Here is your membership card,' he said as he handed it to me. 'You are now an honorary member of the Boys' Club.' I thanked him and looked at the card. It said I was an honorary member. It also said I was entitled to all the rights and privileges of an honorary member. I thought I'd kid him a little so I said, 'What are the rights and privileges of being an honorary member?' He thought a minute and then said, 'I'm not exactly sure, but I suppose that means you have the privilege of donating again next year.' I hope I can do a little better than he did as I try to explain the proposed changes in our by-laws that you are going to vote on."

A memorial service. You might be called on to give the eulogy at a memorial service, speaking about a close friend who has died. Your speech should have a definite opening without a lot of loose, unnecessary talk. It also should have a closing that brings the curtain down on it with no dangling phrases or "thank you's" or awkward apologies. This would make a good opener for such an occasion: "I was honored when I was invited to say a few words about my dear friend. Not being an eloquent speaker, I searched for something that someone more experienced than I had said. I found that, *(#249)* James Russell Lowell once wrote a eulogy of Louis Agassiz. His highest praise of the great naturalist came when he said, 'His magic was not far to seek—he was so human!' And I want to say the same about my friend, 'His magic was not far to seek—he was so human!' "

After you have said what you want about your friend,

you can end your talk with Tennyson's beautiful verse, "Crossing The Bar." *(#642)*

> Sunset and evening star,
>   And one clear call for me.
> And may there be no moaning of the bar,
>   When I put out to sea.
>
> But such a tide as moving seems asleep,
>   Too full for sound and foam,
> When that which drew from out the
>   boundless deep
>   Turns again home.
>
> Twilight and evening bell,
>   And after that the dark!
> And may there be no sadness of
>   farewell
>   When I embark.
>
> For tho' from out our bourne of
>   Time and Place
>   The flood may bear me far,
> I hope to see my Pilot face to face
>   When I have crossed the bar.

You may prefer something simpler and yet something
that will express your sincere depth of feeling. This would be a
fitting close, "I feel much as Horatio did when his friend Hamlet
died. This is what he said: *(#644)* 'His life was gentle and the
elements so mixed in him that nature might stand on its feet and
say to all the world—This was a man.' "

To apologize for an over-crowded room. You might be
acting as the master of ceremonies at a gathering that is
somewhat over-crowded. You can help make people feel better
about the situation with a little humor. Try this: *(#167)*
"The young lady who lives across the street from us was given
one of those little foreign cars for her graduation present.
She was excited about it and pulled into our driveway while I
was mowing the lawn. She was telling me all about the car, and I
said to her. 'It looks mighty tiny. How many will it hold?' 'It's

designed to hold four,' she said, 'but if everybody is well-acquainted and friendly, I can get eight in it.' I know we are a bit over crowded in this room, but I am sure that all of us are well-enough acquainted to enjoy the situation."

If the program is running late. Sometimes, in spite of all you can do, the banquet runs behind schedule. You can adjust this story to fit the circumstances. *(#120)* "A friend of mine is the head of a book publishing company in New York City. Some of his employees live in New Jersey and commute to work. Last winter, during the big blizzard, one of the commuter trains that was taking people home after work, was caught in a snow drift. Everyone on it was stranded overnight. By the middle of the next morning, a path had been cleared so that people could walk to a telephone. One of the publisher's employees called in to the office and said, 'I won't be at work today because I haven't gotten home from work yesterday.' As we start the program, it looks as though we're running a bit late. But I want to assure you that we are going to let you get out of here sometime tonight."

When your voice is not up to par. No matter how careful you are, you might find yourself with a sore throat. You might as well let people know at the very beginning that you have a voice problem. This is one way of getting their attention—and sympathy. Pick up a glass of water and hold it up for all to see and say something like this, "I want to thank the chairman for having this glass of water here for me. This reminds me of the first speech I ever made. *(#152)* I was scared to death. I was afraid nobody would laugh at my funny stories or appreciate my oratory and applaud at the right times throughout my speech. So, just to be sure, I made a deal with a friend of mine. I asked him to come to the meeting and sit on the front row and applaud and laugh at me. I told him that when I took out my handkerchief and wiped my forehead, he was supposed to laugh. And when I took a drink of water, he was supposed to applaud. He said, 'Sure, I'll be glad to be there. But you had better switch those signals because I'll just naturally laugh out loud every time I see you taking a drink of water.' So, you don't have to laugh when you see me take a drink of water. I'm doing it because my throat is a bit hoarse."

As I pointed out earlier, your anecdotes should be tailor-made to fit your speech. They should fit the time, the place, the audience, and the purpose of your talk.

From these examples you can see what a wide open field you have to play on. All you need do, is use your imagination. Visualize your audience. You might even pretend you are sitting in the audience—listening to yourself.

Then build your opening and your closing around a couple of attention-getting anecdotes. Then practice them. When you have done that, you can be sure that your speech will get off to a good start and that your audience will remember what you said when you have finished.

Once you become expert with your openers and closers, you'll find that the middle of your speech will be the easiest part.

CHAPTER 3

How the Experts Do It

ONE OF THE BEST WAYS TO LEARN ANYTHING is to listen to an expert. That applies to public speaking as much as anything else—maybe more, because most public speakers first decided to "try their hand at it" after hearing someone else speak. Some undoubtedly said to themselves, "Hey, I can do better than that. I'm going to try it." Others have said, "What a great speaker—I wish I could speak like that—and maybe if I work at it I can learn to do it."

In putting this book together, I thought it might be well to include a few openers and closers that are used by some of the top professional speakers in America. This isn't quite as good as hearing them in person, but you can certainly see how versatile they are and how much importance they put on their openings and closings.

These examples will show that some like to open with a serious and profound statement. Others open with a touch of humor or even poetry. Their closings are just as carefully planned.

Having been a professional public speaker for more than 30 years, I have heard and become acquainted with many other speakers. I have asked some of them how they open and close their talks. The material included here is quoted exactly the way they gave it to me.

They are not listed in any special order. I hope you enjoy what they have said, and also that you will learn from them.

ARNOLD "NICK" CARTER, Vice-President, Communications Research, Nightingale-Conant Corporation. Nick likes to get the attention of his listeners with a bit of humor. "If you don't mind, I'd like to start off this evening by mentioning the name of John Talbot. Now, you may not have ever heard of the name of John Talbot before . . . and you might not ever hear it again . . . but, tonight, in Dallas, Texas, he's giving a speech. And he said if I'd mention his name, he'd mention mine!"

Nick speaks for only one purpose, to motivate and inspire, whether it is during a seminar or at a banquet. He likes to close with this clincher, "Finally, I'd like to quote the British Bulldog, Sir Winston Churchill, who when he was asked 'what are the most important things to remember when faced with a clutch situation,' said this: 'Never give up. Never . . . give . . . up. NEVER GIVE UP!' And you, baby . . . don't you . . . ever give up!"

MARK C. HOLLIS, Vice-President, Publix Super Markets. He is in great demand by groups of business executives and people in top management. One of his favorite speeches is titled: "An Image Crisis for American Business." He gets his audience's attention by asking an intriguing question, "Have you ever awakened in the middle of the night to the sound of footsteps running outside your bedroom window? It's a frightening experience! You know something is going on out there, but you don't know just what it is and you're not too sure what you ought to do about it. For a minute you lie there perplexed, wondering just what action should be taken."

He then talks about identifying the problem before you can do anything about it. After developing five reasons for what he calls the "identity crisis," he ends his speech with a story designed to get a personal commitment from the listener.

This is his conclusion. "My friends, the answer to the image crisis is not in slogans or creeds, but rests in the hands of business and industrial leaders such as you. Several years ago there was a recluse who lived in the hills of Kentucky. He had a reputation in the small mountain community of being the 'wise old hermit of the hills.' A group of kids got together one day to plan how they could trap the old man. Their plan was simple. They would trap a bird and go up to the hermit's house holding the bird in one of the youngster's hands. They would ask the man if the bird was alive or dead. If he said the bird was dead, the boy would open his hand and allow the bird to fly away. If he said the bird was alive the boy would squeeze the bird between his fingers, open his hand and the bird would be dead. This was a sure thing. The kids caught a bird and tracked up to the 'wise old hermit's' house. As the old man came out to see them, the ringleader asked, 'What is this I have in my hand?' The old sage replied, 'Why son, that's a bird in your hand.' 'True, old man, but is the bird alive or is the bird dead?'

"As the youngsters crowded around, their eyes wide in excitement as they anticipated the opportunity to trap this wise old man, the oldster reached out his hand and gently held the boy's shoulder. He looked him in the eye and said, 'It is as you will it, my son. The answer is in your hands.'

"And as I conclude this evening, I ask you, will you change the image of American business? The answer is in your hands."

MICHAEL AUN, winner in 1978 of first place in the Toastmasters International World Championship of Speaking. He sometimes uses what he calls "The Shhhhhh Opening." He says, "I use this with groups that are loud and often rude. I simply put my finger over my mouth and say sh-h-h-h-h into the microphone to get their attention. If they continue, I continue until someone notices and joins in."

He has one that he calls "The Rubdown Opening." He starts like this, "Everybody on your feet. Now turn to the center isle and put your hands on the shoulders of the person in front of you. [Pause to allow them to get quiet.] Now give them a good rubdown. [Laughter and applause will generally follow.] Okay, be seated. I notice that some of you are taking advantage of the situation. A fellow in the fifth row there. I noticed his hands kept falling gradually. The only problem was it was another man in front of him. Seriously, we do that little exercise for two reasons. First, we want you to get comfortable. And second, I don't know about you, but my underwear rides a little high and I like to readjust it occasionally."

Now and then Mr. Aun uses the technique that was mentioned in the opening chapter, that is, opening and closing with the same words. Here is what he says about it, "I use this quite often when I'm delivering a serious presentation before an intellectual type audience. Many times, I'll open my speech with a quotation and I'll use the same quotation as either a theme or as a closing for the speech. Example, 'This above all: to thine own self be true.' The speech may be built around the quotation or I will close with it, sandwiching the speech in between."

JOE LARSON, President of Sparta Brush Company and Past President of the National Speakers Association. He said to me, "You are so right. The first 30 to 60 seconds are crucial." He went on to explain that time after time he is given a "flowery introduction that is too long." When that happens, he says, he has a number of fast comebacks that are designed to get a laugh and to put the audience at ease. Here are a few that he always has ready, "That was a Burger King introduction . . . one Big Whopper after another." Or, after a short dramatic pause, ". . . And on the 7th day I rested." Or, "I make it a practice after an introduction like that never to say that I don't deserve it because I figure you will find that out soon enough." Or, "If that was all true, you people wouldn't be sitting, you'd be kneeling." Or, "I would rather have talked to you folks last night after your cocktail party because then you were cheerful and jolly and well-adjusted—or in the words of the psychiatrist—all problem drinkers. I'm one. I suffer from Alcoholic Acupuncture . . . I keep getting stuck for the drinks." Or, if the meeting happens to be in a fancy hotel, "The first thing I want to do today is pay tribute to the hotel coffee shop and their religious prices . . . $2.95 for orange juice, $4.25 for two eggs, $1.75 for coffee. I call them religious prices because they remind me of a passage from the Bible, 'I was a stranger and Ye took me in.' "

Mr. Larson says he finds that there aren't as many effective closers as there are openers "because," as he says, "the dramatic closing cannot be too long. But, he has a few favorites.

"And now as you prepare to leave here with faith in your hearts, information in your minds, bills in your pockets and towels in your luggage . . ." Or, "I hope that you will go out of here today determined to be the kind of leader that is expected of you, the competitor you would have yours to be, and most of all, the person your neighbor thinks you are." Or, after he has ended a speech with a poem, he likes to add, "When you give me money, it's only money, but when you give me your time, then you have given me a part of your life. I want to thank each and every one of you for having shared a part of your life with me this evening."

MAXINE McINTYRE, artist, entertainer, and former member of the Board of Directors of the National Speakers Association. She likes to start her presentation with a laugh, and gave this as an example. "Since it is stated in my introduction that I train police officers and narcotic undercover agents, in part of my opening remarks I make it clear to the audience that '*I do not train narcotic agents undercover—but narcotic-undercover agents.*' "

Miss McIntyre is an expert on non-verbal communications, and stresses the importance of "touching" as an important part of communication. To end her presentation on a dramatic note, she relates the story of being raised in a very large, poor farm family and being raised as a non-toucher. She tells how as an adult she could never remember anyone in her family ever affectionately touching her. Then she gives that dramatic punch line, "Tonight when you go home—you *touch* someone you love."

DR. CHARLES W. JARVIS, a dentist from San Marcos, Texas, and recipient of the highest award given by the National Speakers Association. If you never have heard him in person, you will have to imagine him looking over the top of dark-rimmed glasses and warming up his crowd with this rambling sort of beginning. "I want you folks to know right away that I am delighted that the chairman got my name right. I am *not* Howard Jarvis, but Charlie. Not everyone likes Howard. I have found that out any number of times when the emcee inadvertently has introduced me as Howard—even when it is a joke. It was not much of a joke when it was used there at the American Public Works Association meeting in Boston. Those 2,000 people let the boos ring out, for they hate Howard Jarvis. We are certainly no kin. I explained that to them. The man's got hair and money—two things not closely associated with the Jarvises. When that 'Roots' thing came out we wondered about this. I said, 'We.' Mark Twain said a person should never use 'we' unless they are a woman with child or a man with a tapeworm. But, my brother and I—we wondered about our roots. And so we started a deep, genealogical research program. Within three or four months we had our father narrowed down to one of three or four people. So, enough of that."

But, Dr. Jarvis keeps going. He says, "It's wonderful to hear a class introduction. And from a class person. I love class. This is a class audience, too. No one here has asked me to look at their teeth—wonderful. On many occasions people have come up to the head table, have taken out their dentures, their false teeth, and have shown them to me. That's thrilling. I saw lots of those in the dental office—and incidentally, that is the place I prefer to see them. I don't practice now; I did for 12 years, till I started doing this, and some of those sights were not too entertaining—even then."

Since he has his audience with him at this point, he keeps at them with a series of anecdotes. "A guy the other night in Mississippi," he says, "came right up, hauled out his dentures, and that was thrilling—right over my coffee. I don't gag easily, for I *am* a dentist. I still pay my dues, hundreds of dollars a year, for I want to be known as a dentist, and certainly don't want to lose out on the death benefits. When you die, you don't have to pay your dues anymore; those *are* the death benefits. Anyway, this fellow said, 'Thought you'd like to see these teeth, Doc. Made for me by the service. You in the service in the Big War?' 'Yes, sir,' I said. 'Well, you know what I mean, then. See there, in the upper part of my plate, them letters. My name! They put my name in there. Comes in handy, too. Use that to cash a check with.' Don't you know that's a thrill for some teller, just pull 'em out right there in front of her. I told him,

'Sir, in dentistry, that's known as "False Identification." ' I heard some boos then . . . and so help me, that's the last pun I will pull on you. Really that was a test. I was testing the cerebral astuteness of the audience. You see, folks, I am a humorous speaker, not a comic, not a comedian; I am not going to do any pratfalls for you; you're going to have to catch the humor as I lay it on you. And here is something for you to think about: humor is a painful thing told playfully. Interesting, no?"

CONNIE GORDON, an artist and entertainer who puts on "paint parties" where you learn to paint in one hour. When she opens her show, she gets right to the point, "Do you have two left hands? Or can't draw a straight line *with* a ruler? Relax, because I'm going to guide you to paint a masterpiece in this next hour, even if it's your first try!"

An hour later after a hundred or so people have been having fun with their paint brushes, she says, "Be sure to increase your insurance when you get home—because your minds have been made richer by this creative experience. And your home's richer when you display your own original oil painting!"

She opened with a positive statement and a challenge. She closed with a sound claim for success—and happiness.

ROY W. HATTEN, C.P.A.E., another winner of the top award from the American Speakers Association, a magician as well as a motivational speaker. Once when I was on the same program with him, he opened his talk by saying, "Thank you for that gracious introduction. In all of my travels, and being introduced all over the world, I must say in all sincerity, that your introduction is certainly the most recent." When the laughter died down, he gave them another that tore the audience up. He said, "I got out of a sick bed to be here. My secretary has the flu."

He closed with a couple of funny stories that he tied together. They went like this: "I feel like one of you. I don't know which one of you that I feel like, but whoever you are, you should lie down and rest." Then he ended with this one, "Remember, success is not money, position and possessions. It's that warm feeling you get in your heart when *you have* money, position and possessions."

JOE BATTEN, Chairman of the Board of Batten, Batten, Hudson & Swab, Inc., management consultants, lets his audience know he is there to talk about important business. He does not open with any "cutesy or flip" phrases. He gets to the point in his first sentence. "For six thousand years" he says, "we have tried to 'lead' and 'manage' people by 'telling' them what to *do*. Do *you* like to be *told*?"

He then says, "I challenge you to *ask*, *listen*, and *hear*— to try some *new* things—are you *ready*? It's going to take all the manhood or womanhood you can muster! Let's go!"

Joe Batten never lets up. He ends that speech with stirring words like these: "In the beginning, I challenged you to *become* all you can *be*. I'm going to close with these expectations: Armed with a positive *philosophy*, girded with *principles*, guided by *practice*, and sustained by *faith*, resolve to live life to its fullest. Walk tall—with that sure knowledge that the world needs and is hungry for the big, tough-minded individual.

"Do you *care* enough? Only *you* can decide. I love you all!"

RON USELDINGER. President of the Fitness Motivation Institute of America, is another man who gets right down to his subject with straightforward talk. He starts by saying, "I believe fitness and happiness go hand in hand. What makes you happy? What are you committed to in your life? If I were to rank the priorities in my life in order, they would be: (1) Spiritual (2) Physical (3) Family (4) Business. Today, I am going to talk to you about a physical commitment, and how to take better care of your body."

And when he is through motivating you, he closes by saying: "Show me a person who exercises every day, and I will show you someone who feels good about himself. Show me someone who does not exercise, and I will show you someone who feels guilty. We know we need it, but we don't do it. Think about the importance of your body in your life. Is there anything more important here on earth? I don't believe so. Thank you for inviting me here today to share the message with you."

E. LARRY MOLES, who is known as "The Man from Pinch" (West Virginia, that is), likes to capture his audience with a bit of homespun philosophy. And he's good at it. Listen to this opener: "Coming from Pinch, West Virginia, has made it a little difficult for me to adjust to living the way folks do up north—like eating outside and having the bathroom in the house. We do things different in Pinch. Last week I was cooking chicken on my grill. Just minding my own business, turning the spit, when a drunk came around the corner and yelled, 'Sir, you might not know it but your organ ain't playing and your monkey's on fire.'"

While people are laughing at that, he gives them another one, "My son and I went fishing the other day. When we got our campsite ready I told him to go down to the creek and fetch some water. He came running back with an empty bucket. I asked him what the problem was and he replied 'Dad, there's a bear standing in that creek up to his knees in the water.' I said, Son, that bear is just as scared of you as you are of him, and he said, 'Dad, if he is, that water ain't fit to drink.'"

He likes to end his speeches with the same sort of philosophy. Here is one of his favorites: "I'd like to leave you with my recipe for a garden that will be great if you plant it every day. First of all, plant five rows of P's: preparedness, promptness, perseverance, politeness, and prayer. Then plant three rows of squash: squash gossip, squash criticism, and squash indifference. Be sure to plant five rows of lettuce: let us love one another, let us be faithful, let us be loyal, let us be unselfish, and let us be truthful. Of course, no garden would be complete without three rows of turnips: turn up for church, turn up with a new idea, and turn up with the determination to do a better job tomorrow than you did today."

DOTTIE WALTERS, President of Royal Publishers, Inc., is so highly recognized that she served on the Board of Directors of the American Speakers Association. When she talked to me about her work, she said, "I like to begin my speech with a question. My introduction includes so many activities . . . books, newsletters, companies . . . that I like to make fun of myself. 'What did Grandma Moses say when they asked her how she got so much done in 24 hours?' I ask the audience. Then I laugh and say, 'She told them she just *lied* about her age!' Another opener I use: 'Why did God create 25,000 different kinds of beetles? He kept getting a *better idea*. Did you ever get an idea? Did you ever have an idea *hit* you? Raise your hand if it did! Did it ever hit you so hard you grabbed your head?' [Everyone yells yes.] Then I pause a moment, smile and say confidently, 'Well, you are wrong. The idea didn't get you, you got it. Ideas are always in the air, surrounding us. But we have to open the channel of our minds and let the ideas *in*. GENIUS IS A RIVER OF IDEAS."

She says her favorite closing goes like this: "After telling the story of how I began all my businesses by pushing my two babies before me down country roads in one rickety old stroller, to sell advertising . . . telling of my depressing childhood and of a father who told me I was not worth anything . . . and telling of my mother who left me at the library because she could not afford a baby sitter . . . so that I met all the greatest minds who ever lived . . . I say, 'Here is a closing *message* from our cousin, yours and mine . . . who happens to be an ancient Greek, Epictetus:

'When you have darkened your room and
    closed your door,
Do not say that you're alone!
God is within.
Genius is within.
THEY NEED NO LIGHT AT ALL . . .
    To see what we can do.' "

ED FOREMAN, a self-made millionaire at age 26, and the only person in this century to be elected to the U. S. Congress from two different states—Texas and New Mexico. He is famous for what he calls his "Daily Menu" for having "A Terrific Day Everyday!"

He opens that speech this way, "How many of you have a

tendency to worry once in a while?" [He asks for a show of hands.] "If you didn't raise your hand on that one, then you probably didn't understand the question! If you could find out what worry is in one simple sentence and get a sure-fire, fail-safe method of ridding yourself of this troublesome pestilence for the rest of your life, you'd probably want to know about it, wouldn't you."

After that opening, he says, "It's KA-WHAM, and I present the formula for turning worry, frustration and failure into happiness and success." And then he told me, "And it had better be good when you use this kind of opener."

KEN WACKER, insurance executive and a Past Director of the world-wide organization of Rotary International. He is one of the greatest non-clerical inspirational speakers I have ever listened to. He seeks to gain a warm rapport with his audience by starting slowly with a personal experience of some kind.

Even though this opener might take as long as two minutes, people seem eager to hear every word he says, "The year was 1934 and the place was a church in Detroit. I had been invited to 'try out' teaching a high school Sunday school class. This was to be my first audience. When I walked into the room, I was introduced to two rows of wooden folding chairs occupied by what I mistakenly believed would be eager-to-learn young people.

"The superintendent left and I began to read the lesson, and by the way, that's the last lengthy lesson or speech I have ever attempted to read to an audience. As I read, they began crossing and uncrossing their legs in unison somewhat like this." [At this point he steps from behind the lectern and demonstrates with his arms the actions of their legs. He continues this bit of action while explaining that he made up his mind to do three things.]

"First of all, I was going to read every word in that lesson. Secondly, I was not going to let on that their actions bothered me. And finally, I was never coming back again!

"When the class was over and we were leaving, I

overheard one of them say to another, 'We've gotten rid of two others, we won't have any trouble getting rid of this one.'

"That made me mad! So, I came back the next Sunday and the next and the next. And several years ago I concluded a rewarding 30 years of meeting with high school young people on Sunday mornings.

"I'll always be indebted to that young man who thought he had terminated my speaking career at an early stage!"

CLEO DAWSON, Ph.D, noted psychologist and author of the best-selling novel, "She Came to the Valley." I have heard her speak on a number of occasions, and each time she opens with something that pertains specifically to her audience. She seems to have a sixth sense for picking up something to stir her listeners—sometimes with unusual results. She once told me about such an experience.

Her story went like this, "I was invited to speak to 6,000 men and women who were attending a Postmaster's Association meeting at Disneyland in California. I was scared to death when I was introduced because they were all red-hot over a money bill that was pending. I think it had something to do with raising their dues or something like that.

"The room was packed. The place looked like a political convention with all their state banners flying. And I knew the people in the room were divided. Suddenly, I heard myself saying, 'Double the price of postage stamps. No matter what the price, double it! And every citizen in the United States will get earth's biggest bargain—straight from God. Do you know why? Well, I do. Listen!

'I'm a Texan (the Texans clapped). I married a Kentuckian (the Kentuckians clapped). When I was a little girl, I was always away at school—far, far away from Mama—and very lonely. But every day the U.S. Postal Service brought me a letter from Mama down in Texas. And every day I sent Mama a letter from her little girl away at school.

'The price? It wasn't important. It was only a postage stamp. But, that postage stamp brought my mother's love to me. Oh, how I love postage stamps.

'And look at each of you here today—serving on your job. Distance didn't count. You came across the prairies, over mountains, and some of you came from overseas. You flew here. You drove here. You came because you are dedicated to serve—and to deliver those messages of love from one person to another. And the money didn't count.'

"There was deadly silence for one moment, then a stampede of clapping and yelling and waving of banners. Somebody in the crowd shouted, 'I move we pass that money bill.' And somebody else cried out, 'I second the motion.'

"The president stood up and interrupted my speech and said, 'There is a motion on the floor. All in favor say "aye." ' And the bill was passed. As I said, I think they raised their dues.

"I realize that few speeches ever start out like that one, but after that, those people cheered and clapped at everything I said. It was wonderful."

C. CHARLES CHATHAM, S.E.C., President of the Chatham Educational Corporation in Glendale, California. Charles Chatham is a long-time friend of mine who makes three or four speeches a week. I asked him whether or not he ever had occasion to speak at a memorial service for a friend.

He said that he had been called on to offer a eulogy for a member of a trade association of which he was a member. Here is the way he opened his speech, "In each age, in each area, in each activity there are always a few stars that outshine all others.

"The bright glowing of these stars is caused not so much by their own special brilliancy but by their unselfish sharing of that brilliancy. It even appears that the sharing polishes and increases the luminous factor so that it is ever more bright.

"*Giving* has ever been so much more rewarding than *getting*. And giving shines brightly wherever it is constantly practiced—and _____ was a giver. She gave of herself in her own particular way. She gave to individuals, to our Association, to our monthly magazine, and to our profession itself."

He closed his eulogy with these words, "Knowing _____ as well as I did, I know she wants our Association to continue to grow and to keep the flag of our principles flying

high in the morning sun. Those of us who follow her at the helm
are obligated to that cause.

"And we shall not fail her.

"We shall miss her. We do miss her. But we will also
continue to benefit mightily from now on from that very giving
of herself and her talents.

"So, in reality, she really hasn't left us.

"What she was and is, is still with us."

JAMES ARCH, one of the old-timers in the business of
public speaking; a motivator, a man who gets the other fellow
moving; famous for his speech, "Rusting On Your Laurels." He
also teaches public speaking.

He likes to get the attention of his audience in the first
ten seconds of his talk by asking a question. One of his favorites
goes like this: "I would like to ask you a question and get your
response by a show of hands.

How many of you consider yourself to be normal?"

He then pauses and looks around as though he were
counting the hands and says, "That was interesting. We had
some who responded quickly, others looked around and then
decided they should be normal, and then others followed too.
Well, you normals are the ones I need to talk to."

He explains that a successful "show-of-hands" question,
should get a response of 20 percent to 60 percent. "It has many
advantages," he says. "such as getting good participation, relax-
ing the audience and in the case of the above example, it gets a
laugh."

WAYLAND A. TONNING, Ph.D., Professor Emeritus
of Marketing, Memphis State University; author, sales consultant, retired army officer, distinguished public speaker. He
believes in a fast, direct approach to his audience. Listen, "As
the Revolutionary War journalist Thomas Paine used to say,
'We need to be *reminded* much more than we need to be *told*.'
And, in that light, I am not going to tell you anything, but I am
going to remind you of some things you already know and many
of us are inclined to forget."

He likes to end with a humorous story which gives him

the great combination of laughter and applause. This is one he likes to tell, "I have told you my story and now I am in the spot that the girl's father was in. He'd been hanged, and when she was asked, 'How did your father die?' she said, 'He died at a public function when the platform gave way.' So, this platform is getting a bit shaky, thank you and good night."

MISS PATRICIA FRIPP, British businesswoman, author, expert on time management and attitude development, past Director, National Speakers Association, professional public speaker. She has learned to win her audience in the first few seconds before the microphone with these 15 words, "I think it's a great act of faith when people applaud before you do anything!"

WILL KETNER, former radio broadcaster who was famous in Western Pennsylvania some 25 years ago for his "Pee Wee Panel" which was an early morning radio visit into his home with his wife and three kids at the breakfast table. Later, he went into politics and moved to Harrisburg where he works for the State. Among his many humorous openers, this one usually gets his audience in a listening mood.

"I stand before you," he says, "a living example of guilt. I am a bureaucrat. I confess, but ask for your mercy and forgiveness. I come from Harrisburg, where residents of the rural counties will tell you, the Agriculture Department is mobilized, the barns are sterilized, the cows immunized, the milk homogenized, the butter subsidized, the dairymen organized, the milkmen unionized, the price criticized, and the poor farmer is more demoralized than is realized."

At that point he takes a deep breath and goes on, "That's when I worked in the Department of Agriculture. Now, in addition to that, the Department is mobilized, the Gypsy moths need pesticide, the slaughterhouse needs to be purified, the dog kennels sterilized, the race tracks need to be patronized, the matching funds need to be authorized, the marketer is mystified, the customer is demoralized, the farmer is petrified because the whole darn business is computerized."

MIKE FRANK, C.S.P., professional speaker, Past President of the National Speakers Association and owner of Speakers Unlimited, a speakers Bureau. He likes to start with a fast touch of humor, "Thanks, Mr. Chairman, for the kind words of introduction. I guess you covered all the bases but you did forget to indicate that when I was about seven years old, I was president of my neighborhood sandbox." As he says, "That usually gets a chuckle—and sometimes more."

IRA M. HAYES, one of America's greatest sales, motivation and self-improvement speakers; a Past President of the National Speakers Association and famous for his speech, "Keeping Pace With Tomorrow."

Once when he spoke to a huge audience in Canada, he got his audience ready for his message with this lighthearted routine: "I'm glad to be here. A funny thing happened to me last night. The first time I performed in Canada was in the Fall of 1957 and, believe it or not, a man I met out here last night said to me, 'I saw you in 1957.' I said, 'You did?' He said, 'Yeh. What are you doing up here?' And I said, 'I'm going to do a meeting tomorrow morning in here.' 'Oh,' he said, 'you've got another program?' And I said, 'No, it's the same one.'

"A lot of times people will call me and they'll say, 'Hey, we enjoyed your speech at the convention. We have one every year. How about coming back next year and doing another one?' And I say, 'No, I've only got one.'

"It's a lot easier to get a new audience than to get a new program. So, you'll never hear me again. So, stay alert."

SAM EDWARDS, humorist and winner of the coveted CPAE award from the National Speakers Association. He goes to great lengths to start his program with suspense and laughter.

During the banquet, Sam usually leaves the head table a time or two—obviously a little tipsy. When the time comes to introduce him, he is not there. Sometimes, the chairman even has to send someone looking for him. When they finally find him and escort him to the microphone, he looks out over his audience, bewildered for a few seconds, then says, "I have had a few drinks, too." The way he does it, with his excellent sense of timing, tears the audience up. Of course, it might not go over well before a WCTU convention.

JAMES "DOC" BLAKELY, Ph.D., a humorist who speaks on any occasion from a banquet to a three-hour seminar; a past director of the National Speakers Association.

He starts out fast with his humor. Here is one of his best openers: "They told me there were going to be 200-some odd people here. I see there are 200 . . . and some of them are odd. I feel kind of like the guy who had a prepared speech and knew he was going to have to give it to his wife because he forgot his house key. He came in at 3:00 a.m.—stone drunk. Just as he went to knock on the door, she jerked it open. He fell flat on his face, rolled over on one elbow, looked up at her and said, 'I believe I shall dispense with my opening remarks . . . and answer questions from the floor.' "

After 45 minutes or an hour of making his audience laugh, he likes to close with this serious note about humor: "People do not always understand the humorist. That's because we hear the sound of a different drummer. Many times we are not even appreciated because it seems like a rather frivolous occupation for a grown man to follow, going around the country telling wild tales. Just in case you misinterpreted what I've really been saying here tonight, perhaps I can explain it to you in a different way.

"If during the past 45 minutes, you've not once thought of that little nagging problem that you may have brought with you through those doors and especially if you've not once thought of that big problem that I know a certain percentage of you carry as a burden on your heart because of the simple law of statistics, I'll consider our time well-spent and our meeting, as far as my part in it is concerned, to have been a success. If I've made you laugh and you haven't laughed in a while, if I've made you forget, if I've made you consider what great therapy it is not to take yourself so seriously, then I'll consider my time here to have been well-spent.

"Continue to stretch your horizons and let yourself go.

Remember, a grapefruit is just a lemon that had a chance and took it."

ROSS V. HERSEY., C.S.P., motivational humorist who speaks on the need for enthusiasm and excellence. When he gives a speech called, "The Magic Elixir—Enthusiasm," his introduction closes with these words, "He calls himself the King of the Shaggy Dog Story—so what's a shaggy dog story? Here is Ross V. Hersey to tell you."

He starts out this way, "I call myself the King of the Shaggy Dog Story. Perhaps some of you don't know what a shaggy dog story is, so I'll explain. It is usually very long and involved and doesn't have any point to it. And the more ridiculous it is, usually the funnier it is. So let me tell a few of them and by the time I'm finished, I hope you will become addicted to this very strange and different type of humor."

Then, for the next few minutes, before he slips quietly into the serious part of his talk, he tells one story after another. Here is one of his favorites: "Down in Virginia, we tell stories on VPI's, the Hokies of Virginia Tech. They had a real good basketball team this year except for a couple of boys on the team who were kind of dumb. So the coach went to the Dean and said, 'Listen, if I lose these two guys, I'm going to lose the whole year.' So, the Dean went to the professor and said, 'See if you can help the coach out.' So the professor locked these two boys in the classroom and for five days they listened to one record, over and over again, 'Old McDonald Had a Farm.' On Friday afternoon they had an examination consisting of one question. 'If you can answer this question,' the professor said, 'you can play basketball. Old McDonald had a blank. You just fill in that blank, and you'll be all right.' So one of these boys whispered to the other, 'Do you know the answer?' And the other fellow said, 'Yes, I think it's farm.' And the first boy said, 'How do you spell it?' And his friend said, 'E-I-E-I-O.' "

DICK MILHAM, one of America's top speakers in the field of sales motivation, a specialist in real estate, humorous and entertaining. His best openings contradict the quick opening technique. He likes to take his time to set the stage for his talk but he has no trouble holding his audience as he opens with a story. Here is one of his favorites.

"You can lose perspective in life. You can focus on all you don't have to the extent you lose sight of all you do possess. You can focus in on what others gain and become greedy for it all. One of the keys to a successful personal and business life is the ability to share with others. To share your knowledge, your skills, your advice without concern for how it will benefit you. This is giving for the sake of giving. The alternative is simple. To hide yourself in the wraps of your own narrow world. At a recent meeting I was told that one of the leading salesmen in the nation was unwilling to appear on the program because 'I don't want everyone else to find out how I'm doing it . . . why should I train my competition?'

"And so a story . . . an ancient story that surfaces from the antiquity of my people: [Dick Milham is of Lebanese extraction.]

"Two shepherders were caring for their flocks when they heard the screams of a man in desperate trouble. They ran toward the river and saw a figure struggling in the rapid water, being dragged to his death. One of the men dove into the water and the other threw a line in front of them. The rescue was made. As the old man lay on the ground he made a startling statement: 'You have shown courage and I have the power to give you a great gift. Either of you may wish for anything you desire and you will get it and the other of you will receive twice as much.'

"At first the two men thought the old man might be crazy, but after he left them they decided that if he did have that power, they should be careful and take it seriously. One of them turned to the other and said, 'You go ahead and wish.'

"He started to and then remembered 'the other will get twice as much' and he said, 'No you go ahead and wish first.'

"At first it was like a game. Kidding each other about the wealth . . . but as the days went on it became more serious. One of them would think . . . I'd like a mountain of gold . . . and start to wish . . . and then he would feel that nagging, 'but if I do, he will get two mountains . . .'

"The other thought, 'an ocean of diamonds . . . but if I do, he gets two oceans . . .' And so the focus changed . . . from all that they could have to what the other would gain.

"So the tension grew . . . and the friendship crumbled . . . and the anger increased until late one night, one of them woke up and could take it no longer. He crept over to the form of the other man sleeping and suddenly grabbed his throat and started choking him and screaming . . . 'WISH, WISH or I'll kill you. WISH!'

"And in that moment, the startled man looked into the hate-filled face of his one-time friend and gasped with his dying breath . . . 'I WISH . . . I WISH . . . to be made blind in my right eye.'

"And so he was made blind in his one eye . . . and the other in BOTH EYES . . . cursed to stumble in darkness the rest of his life.

"GREED DESTROYS!"

CHARLIE and MARTHA SHEDD, the most famous husband and wife writing and speaking team in America. Always together, they write books and hold seminars on all sorts of family problems. Sometimes they talk to adults and sometimes to teenagers.

They have developed a number of techniques for getting their audience to participate. Their favorite is to start with a provocative question. For example, when they are opening a marriage workshop and want to get into the subject of hostility, they often start like this, "Do you ever feel your mate is pushing you around?"

They follow that up by reading a letter from their bottomless store of correspondence that focuses directly on that theme. From that fast beginning, they capture their audience and the questions come in an endless flow.

When they talk to a youth group, their question often is, "How do you rate yourself as a quality person, genuine beauty, real class . . . how do you grade yourself from zero to one hundred, with seventy for passing?" They have yet to encounter a non-participating, non-interested, non-responsive audience.

CHAPTER 4

Openers

THIS CHAPTER CONTAINS 421 OPENERS. Some are humorous. Some are serious. All of them have been used successfully at one time or another to get a speaker's speech off to a fast start.

They will work for you, too, if you will study the examples and follow the suggestions given in Chapter 2.

With that in mind, we're going to pretend we're preparing a speech. We will look at two or three imaginary audiences, search out an opener or two for each one, then rewrite them to fit.

So, let's put on our thinking caps, polish off our imaginations, and exercise a little ingenuity.

We might as well start with Story #1.

When you first read it, you may wonder, "How in the world can anybody use that as an opener for a speech? It doesn't seem to relate to anything." And you'd be right if you stood before your audience and read it exactly as it is written.

But, look how one speaker used it. He was going to talk on certain aspects of the economy, and his speech required that he quote a number of statistics. He walked to the lectern with a handful of notes.

To put his audience at ease, he used Story #1 and said something like this, "You will notice that I have a few notes in front of me. I brought them to keep me from absent-mindedly

wandering down the wrong track when I speak. I had a friend
who used to do that. In fact, he was about as absent-minded as
anyone you ever saw.

"One night he came home late from some sort of meeting.
He had put on his pajamas and was getting into bed when he
looked at the woman who already was in the bed. 'Lady, what
are you doing in my bed?' he said.

" 'Well,' she said, 'I like this bed. I like this neighborhood. I like this house. I like this room. Besides, I'm your
wife.' "

That example shows how any of these stories can be
made to fit if you put your mind to the task.

Now, suppose you are looking for openers you can use
for a specific occasion—say, a retirement dinner for your sales
manager.

Although you may want to kid him and turn the occasion
into a gentle roast, you might want to start with a genuine
compliment. Why not look under the word "Success." There you
find a great quotation by Phillips Brooks. *(#384).* Use it this
way. "More than a hundred years ago, Phillips Brooks said, 'To
find his place and fill it is success for a man.' Tonight we come to
pay honor to a man who found his place and filled it—filled it
with enthusiasm, with determination, and persistence—Joe
Blow."

With that sort of start, you can say some other good
things about him—his great record with the company and so on.
Then you weave in a bit of humor. Since he is retiring as your
sales manager, look under Salesmanship.

Try *#348*, and tell it on Joe something like this. "Joe had
his own way of keeping his salesmen on their toes and helping
them to produce. I remember those sales contests he used to run
for the men. One time when he started a new contest, he called a
sales meeting and said, 'Today, we're announcing the biggest
sales contest we have ever put on. It will run for eight weeks
and each man will be given a quota for that period of time.'

"One of the salesman raised his hand and said, 'What do
you get if you make your quota?' And Joe told him. 'You get to
keep your job.' "

You won't want to stop with only one laugh, so you look under the cross-references at the end of the Salesmanship category. You'll find three; and decide you like *#294*. Make it fit Joe by saying, "Joe owes much of his success to being able to see things from the customer's point of view. I think he learned that long before he came to work for us. One of his first jobs was selling fishing tackle in a sporting goods store. One day he was showing his friend his line of artificial bait. He showed him a bright yellow lure and said, 'This is our best seller.' His friend looked at it and said, 'That sure is a bright looking plug. But, I wouldn't think a bass would strike at such an outlandish looking thing.'

" 'You may be right,' Joe said, 'but I don't sell them to the fish. I sell them to people.' "

How about one more for Joe? Turn to the Thematic Index for Openers. There you will find hundreds of ideas listed with the story number. You check through half a dozen of them without finding one you can adapt. Then you see an entry for "Lifetime Contract." You think that might apply to a man who is retiring. The number of the story is *#257*. This one calls on you to use your imagination and ingenuity. So, you tell it like this:

"When Joe said he wanted to retire, we were disappointed. We hated to think of losing him, so I suggested that he stay on. I even offered him a lifetime contract. He turned it down, and I asked him why.

" 'Well,' he said, 'I had a friend who was given a lifetime contract. He was happy about it for three or four years and then he got a new boss. That boss didn't like him so one day he called my friend in and declared him legally dead and fired him.' "

That opening routine should get your meeting off to a great start. The principle is simple—make your story fit! Make it sound like the truth!

Here's another example. You are speaking to a group of young people who are members of 4-H or Future Farmers or Junior Achievement. You want to get their attention right away, but you also want to give them something serious to think about.

You look under "Advice" in this section and find story

#5. Tell it like this. "When I was invited to speak tonight I asked Mr. Chairman what he wanted me to say. He said I should give you some helpful advice for your future. Now, that's hard to do because young people don't like to hear advice.

"I'm reminded of the young man who had just reached the age of 21 and his parents had given him a big birthday party and a new car. 'Now that you are a man,' his father said, 'you will be earning your own money and going your own way. But, I'd like to give you a final word of advice. Don't go wild with your new freedom. For example, don't start hanging out in those topless bars that you read about.'

" 'Why not?' his son said.

" 'I'll tell you why not,' his father said. 'For one thing, you'll see a lot of things that you shouldn't see.'

"But as all young people do, his son ignored his father's advice and the next night he went to a topless bar. And his father was right. He saw something there that he should not have seen—his father."

You have now set the scene for a bit of serious advice—something that you could even use as the theme of your speech.

"Now, let me give you some good advice. It's some of the best advice ever given to young people who plan to accomplish something in life. I did not originate it. It comes from a great philosopher by the name of Johann Wolfgang von Goethe who lived more than 150 years ago. *(#52)* This is what he said:

> 'Are you in earnest? Seize this very minute:
> What you can do, or dream you can, begin it;
> Boldness has genius, power, and magic in it.
> Only engage, and the mind grows heated;
> Begin and then the work will be completed.' "

And there you are. Every story in this book could be used as an example. But to do that would restrict the boundaries of your mind. It would build a fence around your imagination.

So, from here on, you are on your own.

After all, these are now *your stories*. Use them—with eagerness, with enthusiasm and with vivacity.

The Openers

ABSENT MINDED

1. The absent-minded professor had put on his pajamas and was getting into his bed when he looked at the woman who already was in the bed. "Lady, what are you doing in my bed?" he asked.

"Well," she said, "I like this bed. I like this neighborhood. I like this house. I like this room. Besides, I'm your wife."

ACTION

2. In every affair consider what precedes and what follows, and then undertake it.

–Epictetus

121, 336.

ADDRESS

3. Once at a banquet when half a dozen speakers had said "a few words" and the golf trophies had been passed out and the clock was ready to strike 11:00 o'clock, the master of ceremonies said, "Now ladies and gentlemen, here is the moment we have been waiting all evening for. Mr. Gene Murphy will now give us his address."

Mr. Murphy walked to the lectern and said, "Thank you Mr. Chairman. My address is 6320 Pat Avenue, Canoga Park, California 91303. Please write to me sometime."

ADVENTURE

4.   Did you ever notice how people think? When they are at home sitting in their favorite chair in front of the fireplace, they wish they were in some faraway place having an adventure. And when they are in a faraway place in the middle of an adventure, they wish they were back home sitting in front of a warm fire.

ADVICE

5.   The young man had just reached the age of 21 and his parents had given him a big birthday party and a new car. "Now that you are a man," his father said, "you will be earning your own living and going your own way. But, I'd like to give you a final word of advice. Don't go wild with your new freedom. For example, don't start hanging out in those topless bars that you read about."

"Why not?" his son asked.

"I'll tell you why not," his father said. "For one thing, you'll see a lot of things that you shouldn't see."

But as all young people do, his son ignored his father's advice and the next night he went to a topless bar. And his father was right. He saw something there that he should not have seen—his father.

6.   The guest speaker was getting out of a taxi in front of the town hall where he was to address an international convention. As he finished paying the taxi driver and turned to enter the building, he was stopped by a panhandler who said to him, "Excuse me sir, would you please give me two or three bucks so I can get something to drink?"

"What?" the speaker said. "I never heard of such a thing. That's no way to beg for money."

"Look, bud," the panhandler said, "I don't tell you how to make a speech so don't you tell me how to run my business."

7.   The judge had assigned a young attorney to defend a suspect in a burglary. "This will be good experience for you," the judge said. "I want you to give your client the best advice you can. Be ready for his trial one week from today."

A week later when the judge called up the case, he said to the lawyer, "Are you ready to go to trial? Is your client in court?"

"No, sir, he's not here, your honor," the young lawyer said. "You told me to give him the best advice I could think of so I told him to take off for Mexico."

8.   The newspaper reporter was interviewing a celebrity, one of the world's most famous hotel owners. As a final question, he said to the great man, "Millions of travelers from all over the world have stayed in your hotels. I wonder if you have a word of advice that you would like to pass on to them?"

"Yes, I have," the great hotel man said. "Please keep the shower curtain *inside*."

118.

AGE

9.   An elderly man who thought he was a lady's man was flirting with the pretty waitress one morning at breakfast. He started out with the world's oldest cliché, "Darling, where have you been all my life?"

"Well," she said with a pretty smile, "for the first 45 years of it, I wasn't even born yet."

10.   It gives me great pleasure to converse with the aged. They have been over the road that all of us must travel, and know where it is rough and difficult and where it is level and easy.

–Plato

11.   To know how to grow old is the masterwork of wisdom, and one of the most difficult chapters in the great art of living.

–Henri-Frederic Amiel

12.   Whenever a man's friends begin to compliment him about looking young, he may be sure that they think he is growing old.

-*Washington Irving*

39.

AGRICULTURE

13.   Agriculture is the most useful of the occupations of man.

-*Thomas Jefferson*

148, 150.

AIRPLANE

14.   I'm happy to be here this evening. My plane arrived on time and I had no delays. I even checked into the hotel in time to take a nap. The airlines in America are great. The other day I had a speech in San Francisco. I arrived in time with no trouble, but my baggage was in Dallas.

AMBITION

15.   The world owes all its onward impulses to men ill at ease. The happy man inevitably confines himself within ancient limits.

-*Nathaniel Hawthorne*

AMERICA

16.   If we are going to continue to be proud that we are Americans there must be no weakening of the codes by which we have lived; by the right to meet your accuser face to face, if you have one; by your right to go to church or the synagogue or

even the mosque of your own choosing; by your right to speak your mind and be protected in it.

–Dwight D. Eisenhower

17.   The things that will destroy America are prosperity-at-any-price, peace-at-any-price, safety-first instead of duty-first, the love of soft living and the get-rich-quick theory of life.

–Theodore Roosevelt

18.   America cannot be an ostrich with its head in the sand. America cannot shut itself out from the rest of the world.

–Woodrow Wilson

246.

AMERICAN

19.   Americans are great "joiners," great "card carriers." But among the lodge, union, social security, credit, medicare and other cards we carry in our wallets, you won't find the kind which must be carried at all times by people in other countries—a police state identification card.

–Author Unknown

ANGER

20.   Anybody can become angry—that is easy; but to be angry with the right person, and to the right degree, and at the right time, and for the right purpose, and in the right way—that is not within everybody's power and is not easy.

–Aristotle

21.   When I am angry I can write, pray, and preach well, for then my whole temperament is quickened, my understanding sharpened, and all mundane vexations and temptations depart.

–Martin Luther

275.

ANSWERS

22. The candidate had finished his formal speech and was conducting a question-and-answer period. "I will do my best to answer any of your questions," he said, "but I must remind you that even though I am familiar with all of the principal questions of the day, I do not know all of the answers."

APPLAUSE

23. Thank you for that warm round of applause. I sure do wish you had been in the audience where I spoke three nights ago.

382.

ARCHITECT

24. A man was in deep consultation with the architect who was designing his new home. The architect was having a hard time understanding just what type of house the man wanted. "Can't you give me some idea of the style or period that you would like?" he asked.

"I'm sorry," the man said. "All I know is that my wife wants something that will go with an antique brass doorknocker that she bought last summer in Virginia."

ARGUMENT

25. A man was being interviewed for a job. The personnel director asked him why he had left his previous employment.

"I couldn't stand the way the sales manager and the bookkeeper were always arguing. It went on all day, every day. and I just got tired of it."

"That must have been an unpleasant experience," the personnel director said.

"Yes it was," the prospective employee said. "They were at it all the time. If it wasn't me and the sales manager, it was me and the bookkeeper."

26.   There is no good in arguing with the inevitable. The only argument available with an east wind is to put on your overcoat.

‑James Russell Lowell

ART

27.   One picture in ten thousand, perhaps, ought to live in the applause of mankind, from generation to generation until the colors fade and blacken out of sight or the canvas rots entirely away.

‑Nathaniel Hawthorne

115.

ASSIGNMENT

28.   The topic that your program chairman asked me to talk about this evening covers a wide range of knowledge and experience. Although I do know something about the subject, I must admit that my familiarity with it is limited. But my imagination is not limited. And so I ask you to bear with me when I am forced to draw on my imagination, when I don't know what I am talking about.

ASTRONAUTS

29.   As the plane bringing the guest of honor and his wife to the convention came into the airport to land, the pilot's voice came over the intercom and said, "Ladies and gentlemen, just a few moments ago a rocket took off from the Kennedy Space Center. It was a perfect launch and the astronauts will be circling the earth once every 90 minutes. We are living in a marvelous age."

After leaving the plane and walking for a quarter of a

mile through the terminal, and waiting 20 minutes for their baggage, and another 20 minutes for a taxi, they finally arrived at the hotel. After a further delay, while they checked in and were escorted to their room, the man looked at his watch and said to his wife. "Like the man on the plane said, We live in a marvelous age. From the time it took us to get off the plane and get into our room, those astronauts have already been around the world."

ATHLETICS

30.   Competition in play teaches the love of the free spirit to excel by its own merit. A nation that has not forgotten how to play, a nation that fosters athletics is a nation that is always holding up the high ideal of equal opportunity for all. Go back through history and find the nations that did not play and had no outdoor sports and you will find the nations of oppressed peoples.

–Warren G. Harding

AUTHOR

31.   Following his lecture to a group of college students, the famous author was bombarded with questions by would-be writers. "What is your secret formula for writing?" one student asked.

"It really isn't a secret," the author said. "All you have to do is put a sheet of blank paper in the typewriter and write down the words as they come to you."

"That sounds as though writing is easy," the student said.

"Oh, it is, it is," the great author said. "The writing part is easy. It's getting the words to come to you that's difficult."

32.   The inexperienced author sent his first novel to a publisher with a notation which said, "The characters in this book are purely fictitious and bear no resemblance whatever to anyone living or dead."

A week later he received his manuscript back. The editor had written beneath the author's note, "That's exactly what is wrong with it."

33.   The author who was invited to speak at a Thanksgiving dinner opened his speech by saying, "For the past half-hour you have been giving your attention to a turkey stuffed with sage. Now I hope you will give your attention to a sage stuffed with turkey."

34.   I don't want to be a doctor, and live by men's diseases; nor a minister to live by their sins; nor a lawyer to live by their quarrels. So I don't see there's anything left for me but to be an author.

–Nathaniel Hawthorne

35.   The public speaker turned author was eagerly reading a review of his first book. "This book" said the critic, "is not to be read and lightly tossed aside. It should be thrown with great force."

36.   He that publishes a book runs a very great hazard, since nothing can be more impossible than to compose one that may secure the approbation of every reader.

–Miguel de Cervantes Saavedra

37.   The author who speaks about his own books is almost as bad as a mother who talks about her own children.

–Benjamin Disraeli

335, 367.

AUTHORITY

38.   The sign at a municipal parking lot said, "All day parking $2.00."

A man who worked in a nearby office parked there one morning and at noon he asked the attendant if he could take his

car out of the lot, drive to a restaurant for lunch, and return it
for the rest of the day without paying an additional charge.

The attendant said, "No, sir. That may sound reason-
able, but I have to get $2.00 every time a car drives in the lot.
Those are the rules and I can't change the rules. I'm not on the
policy-making level."

BAD NEWS

39.   Two housewives who were friends decided they would
go back to work now that their children were grown. They went
together to apply for employment at a large manufacturing
plant.

They were sitting side by side as they filled in the long
and detailed application forms. As one of the women came to the
little box marked "age," she sat staring out of the window as
though in deep thought.

Her friend leaned over and whispered, "Go ahead and
put it down. The longer you wait, the worse it gets."

BALDNESS

40.   A speaker who was nearly totally bald, said to his audience, "I want to say that of all my childhood dreams, one of them
has come true. When I was little, and my mother used to sham-
poo my hair and then make me comb it every morning, I said I
wish I didn't have any. Now look at me."

BALLOT

41.   The ballot is stronger than the bullet.

–Abraham Lincoln

BANKING

42.   I sincerely believe that banking establishments are more
dangerous than standing armies, and that the principle of spend-

ing money to be paid by posterity, under the name of funding, is but swindling futurity on a large scale.

–Thomas Jefferson

BASEBALL

43.   A young fellow was taking his new girlfriend to see her first baseball game. Because of heavy traffic they did not arrive until the middle of the fourth inning. "What's the score?" the young man asked one of the fans as they were settling into their seats.

"Nothing to nothing, last half of the fourth," the fan said.

"Oh, that's good," said the young fellow's girlfriend, "even though we were late getting here, we haven't missed a thing."

BEGINNING

44.   The trip was long and the bus was crowded. After a few miles the passenger, who obviously had been drinking, reached into the small bag which he had placed under his seat and removed a pint of whiskey. He studied the bottle for a moment then took a long swig from it.

His action could not be ignored by the man sitting next to him who said, "I'm 65 years old, and in my entire life I never have taken a drink of whiskey."

As the man with the bottle carefully screwed the cap back on it and returned it to his bag, he said rather scornfully, "Well, one thing's for sure, you sure aren't going to start now."

BELIEF

45.   I am proud of the revolutionary beliefs for which our forebears fought . . . the belief that the rights of man come not from the generosity of the state but the hands of God.

–John F. Kennedy

BENEVOLENCE

46.   Benevolence never developed a man or a nation. We do not want a benevolent government. We want a free and a just government.

–Woodrow Wilson

BIBLE

47.   The Bible is the best book in the world. It contains more of my little philosophy than all the libraries I have seen; and such parts of it as I cannot reconcile to my little philosophy, I postpone for future investigation.

–John Adams

BIRTHDAY

48.   A man was talking to a friend and said, "My son's seventeenth birthday is next week, and if I give him everything he asked for, it's going to cost me a couple of hundred dollars."

His friend said, "That's one thing you can say for my boy. He was seventeen years old three months ago and the gift he asked for cost me only seventy-five cents."

"What in the world could you buy for only seventy-five cents that would satisfy any normal seventeen-year-old boy," the man asked.

"Oh," his friend said. "That was easy. I gave him his own set of keys to the car."

BLESSINGS

49.   How little do my countrymen know what precious blessings they are in possession of, and which no other people on earth enjoy.

–Thomas Jefferson

235.

BOLDNESS

50.   Tender-handed stroke a nettle,
       And it stings you for your pains;
     Grasp it like a man of mettle,
       And it soft as silk remains.

51.   Unless you enter the tiger's den, you cannot take the cubs.

–Old Japanese Proverb

52.   Are you in earnest? Seize this very minute:
     What you can do, or dream you can, begin it;
     Boldness has genius, power, and magic in it.
     Only engage and the mind grows heated;
     Begin and then the work will be completed.

–Johann Wolfgang von Goethe

156, 158.

BOOK

53.   The first time I read an excellent book, it is to me just as if I had gained a new friend. When I read over a book I have perused before, it resembles the meeting with an old one.

–Oliver Goldsmith

54.   It is chiefly through books that we enjoy intercourse with superior minds . . . In the best books, great men talk to us, give us their most precious thoughts, and pour their souls into ours.

–William Ellery Channing

55.   No book is so bad but some profit may be gleaned from it.

–Pliny the Elder

56.   It is a great thing to start life with a small number of really good books which are your very own.

–Sir Arthur Conan Doyle

36, 37, 47, 70, 268, 367.

BOXING

57.   A man who tried never to miss a boxing match on television had an important business meeting the night the championship bouts were going to be televised. He hated to miss seeing the fight but he did what he thought was the next best thing. He asked his wife to watch for him and tell him the result when he got home.

When the meeting was over and he came in the front door, he said, "Well, honey, how did the championship fight come out? Who won?"

"Nobody won," she said. "One of the men got hurt in the first round and fell down unconscious so they had to quit."

BRAGGING

58.   Several kids were bragging about how tough they were.

The first little boy said, "I'm so tough that I can wear out a pair of shoes in six weeks."

"That's nothing," the second little boy said. "I'm so tough that I can wear out a pair of dungarees in six days."

But the little girl from next door had the best one. She said, "You two aren't so tough. I can wear out my grandmother in six minutes."

37, 44, 154, 413.

BREVITY

59.   The little second-grader's family had just moved and she was going to her new school for the first time. When she came home that afternoon she said to her mother, "What's sex?" Her mother had been expecting that question for some time and she was ready for her tiny daughter. So, for the next half hour she explained about the birds and the bees. Then she said to her, "Now, do you understand what I have been telling you?" "Yes," her daughter said, "I think I do." Then she showed her mother a school registration card that she had brought home from school and said. "But, how am I going to get all of that into this little square?"

60.   A fashion commentator said, "A dress should always be tight enough to show that there is a woman in it. And it should be loose enough to let everybody know that she is a lady."

BUREAUCRACY

61.   Bureaucracy is ever desirous of spending its influence and its power. You cannot extend the mastery of the government over the daily working life of a people without at the same time making it the master of the people's souls and thoughts.

–Herbert Hoover

BUSINESS

62.   The business of the country is like the level of the ocean, from which all measurements are made of heights and depths.

–James A. Garfield

63.   A small-town banker was telling a friend how he got started in the banking business some 40 years before.

"I was out of work" he said. "So, to keep busy, I rented an empty store and painted the word BANK on the window. That very first day a man came in and put in $200. The next day a little lady came in and gave me $100 and that same afternoon a fellow deposited $400. By the third day, I'd got so much confidence in the project that I put in $50 of my own money."

64.   Commerce has made all winds her messengers; all climes her tributaries; all her people her servants.

–Tryon Edwards

166, 332, 405.

CAMPAIGN

65.   Before I begin my speech, I want to say how touched I am to be invited to speak at this campaign dinner. But, considering that each of you had to pay $1,000, I must say that I am not quite as touched as you were.

CANDIDATE

66.   The candidate said to the voter, "Well, can I count on your vote next Tuesday?"

"Not this time," the voter said. "But, I've got you down as my second choice."

"Who's your first choice?" the candidate asked.

"Anybody else who is running," the voter said.

97, 374.

CAREER

67.   The little fellow's father had been bragging about him. "Someday he's going to be a great politician," he said.

"He's only three years old," the man's friend said. "How do you know he's going to be a politician?"

"Because," the boy's father said, "he never stops talking. And even though the things he says don't make any sense, he sure can make them sound good."

CAT

68.   A kitten had strayed into the kindergarten class and the children were having great fun playing with it. After a while one of the little girls asked the teacher whether it was a girl cat or a boy cat.

The teacher didn't want to get into that subject with the little ones so she said, "I don't think I can tell."

"I know how we can tell," one little boy said, "We can vote on it."

CAUSE

69. All human actions have one or more of these seven causes: chance, nature, compulsion, habit, reason, passion, and desire.

–Aristotle

CENSORSHIP

70. I am . . . mortified to be told that, in the United States of America . . . a question about the sale of a book can be carried before the civil magistrate . . . Are we to have a censor whose imprimatur shall say what books may be sold, and what we may buy? . . . Whose foot is to be the measure to which ours are all to be cut or stretched? . . . Shall a layman, simple as ourselves, set up his reason as the rule for what we are to read? . . . It is an insult to our citizens to question whether they are rational beings or not.

–Thomas Jefferson

CERTAINTY

71. If a man will begin with certainties, he will end with doubts; but if he will be content to begin with doubts, he shall end in certainties.

–Francis Bacon

72.   No great deed is done
        By falterers who ask for certainty.

—George Eliot

CHANGE

73.   There is a certain relief in change, even though it be
from bad to worse; as I have found in traveling in a stagecoach,
it is often a comfort to shift one's position and be bruised in a
new place.

—Washington Irving

74.   Change is inevitable in a progressive country. Change is
constant.

—Benjamin Disraeli

75.   There is danger in reckless change, but greater danger
in blind conservatism.

—Henry Glasgow

103.

CHARITY

76.   Charity is not just giving a dog a bone. It is giving a dog
a bone when you are as hungry as the dog.

169, 170.

CHILDREN

77.   Do you know where your kids are tonight?

37.

CHINA

78.   A man was asked to address a meeting of the Ladies' Literary Guild. The program chairman asked him to speak on the topic of China and Chinese art, religion and philosophy. He spent several long nights in research studying for his presentation. When he arrived at the meeting place on the great day, he said to the chairman, "I suppose you wanted me to speak about China because you are making a study of their early culture, is that right?

"No," the chairman said, "we just wanted your topic to be appropriate for today's luncheon. You see, we're going to serve Chop Suey."

CHOICE

79.   A second lieutenant at an army base had been given the job of organizing a dance at the officers club. He was in the process of calling various civic organizations in town asking that they help line up young ladies for the big affair. He called the dean at a local teachers college and asked if she could arrange to have some of her students there.

"I think that would be nice," the dean said. "I'll make sure that ten of our most upright and proper young ladies attend."

The young lieutenant thanked her profusely and then said, "Instead of doing that, how about sending five of that kind and five of the others?"

80.   The young junior high student was studying about politics. "Dad," he asked his father, the mayor, "what do you call a fellow who leaves your political party and goes over to the other side."

"He's a traitor, son, a political traitor," the boy's father said.

"Well, what would you call someone who deserts the other party and comes over to your side?" the boy asked.

"I'd call him a man of rare judgment, a man who knows his own mind and a political convert," the boy's father said.

66, 233, 306, 344, 410.

CHRISTMAS

81.   A man bought a bottle of whiskey to give his yard man for Christmas. He bought the cheapest whiskey he could find. It was about the worst whiskey on the market. He gave it to the man for Christmas and two weeks later when the man came to work on his yard he said, "I sure do want to thank you for that liquor. It was exactly right."

"What do you mean when you say it was exactly right?" the man asked.

The yard man said, "Well, if it had been any better you wouldn't have given it to me and if it had been any worse I couldn't have drunk it."

82.   A couple of weeks before Christmas, when a businessman went to pick up his car in the building's parking garage, he found a card under the windshield wiper of his car. "Merry Christmas," it said, "from all the fellows in the parking garage."

Since he always parked his own car and picked it up himself, he saw no need to tip anyone. But, someone else felt differently about that. Because a week later another card on his windshield read, "Merry Christmas from all the fellows in the parking garage—second notice."

83.   After those glowing words of introduction from Mr. Chairman, I hope you don't get the same impression of me that my little nephew did last Christmas. I was invited to play the part of one of the three Magi in a nativity scene at our church. One of his friends asked him if his father was going to be in the play. He said, "No, my father isn't, but my uncle is."

"What part is he going to play?" his friend asked.

And my nephew said, "He's one of the Wise Guys from the East."

84.   I have always thought of Christmas time when it has come round, as a good time; a kind, forgiving, charitable time; the only time I know, in the long calendar of the year, when men and women seem by one consent to open their shut-up hearts freely, and to think of people below them as if they really were fellow passengers to the grave, and not another race of creatures bound on other journeys.

–Charles Dickens

85.   The height of the automated age was reached when a man stepped on an automatic elevator. As soon as he punched the button for his floor, a voice came over the speaker saying, "This is your automated elevator wishing you a Merry Christmas."

CIVILIZATION

86.   The true test of civilization is not the census, nor size of cities, nor the crops, but the kind of man that the country turns out.

–Ralph Waldo Emerson

CLARITY

87.   A directive from the Department of Defense was sent to all Army units in the field. It read: "It is necessary for technical reasons that these warheads must be stored upside down, that is, with the top at the bottom and the bottom at the top. To prevent anyone making a mistake, and in order that there will be no doubt as to which is the bottom and which is the top, for storage purposes, it will be noted that the bottom of each warhead has been labeled with the word 'Top.' "

60.

COMMENT

88.   When the banquet was over and the audience was leaving the room, a woman said to her husband, "Oh, wasn't that an inspirational speaker?"

"As far as I'm concerned," he said, "thirty minutes of rain would have done us more good."

355.

COMMERCE

89.   Commerce is the great civilizer. We exchange ideas when we exchange fabrics.

–Robert Green Ingersoll

64, 404.

COMMON SENSE

90.   If a man can have only one kind of sense, let him have common sense. If he has that and uncommon sense too, he is not far from genius.

–Henry Ward Beecher

COMMUNICATION

91.   A church installed a set of electronic chimes, the kind that work from a tape and with speakers that have adjustable volume control. The plan was to mount the speakers in the tower of the church and play sacred music every Sunday afternoon. To make sure that they were not playing too loud, several teams from the church checked with the people in the neighborhood during the first concert. One of the deacons rang a doorbell and the lady of the house came to the door.

The deacon said, "I'm here from the . . ."

"What did you say?" the woman asked.

"I said I am here from the church, and . . ."

And the lady said, "I'm sorry but you'll have to talk louder. I can't hear a word you are saying on account of those darn chimes."

92.   I consider it a high honor to be invited to speak to you young people on this great occasion. I hope I will be able to say something that will be of help to you. However, there is one problem that I can't help you with. All I can do is warn you about it. This is it: 20 years from now you are going to be faced with the difficult problem of communicating with your own teen-age children.

COMPLIMENT

93.   Several weeks ago after I had spoken at a banquet, I was standing with the president of the association at the door of the dining room shaking hands with the people as they were leaving. Everyone had something nice to say about my speech until that last man who finally shook my hand. As he did, he said, "I think that was the worst speech I ever heard and whoever invited you to speak tonight should be put out of the organization."

Of course, I was embarrassed. But the president was the one who got upset. He said to me, "Don't pay any attention to what that fellow said. He's considered to be a half-wit. He's never had an original thought in his life. He's nothing but a copycat. All he does is stand around listening to what other people say and then repeats it everywhere he goes."

94.   The other night after I had spoken to a rather large crowd at dinner, I was milling around with people in the lobby of the hotel. I wasn't exactly eavesdropping, but I did overhear a woman say to her husband, "Oh, that speaker tonight. I'm so full of his message that I can hardly speak."

And her husband said, "I know exactly how you feel, I got a bellyfull of him myself."

101, 219, 335.

COMPROMISE

95.   We learned once and for all that compromise makes a good umbrella but a poor roof; that it is a temporary expedient, often wise in party politics, almost sure to be unwise in statesmanship.

–James Russell Lowell

COMPROMISE

96.   All government—indeed, every human benefit and enjoyment, every virtue and every prudent act—is founded on compromise and barter.

–Edmund Burke

CONGRESSMAN

97.   The Congressman's wife was going with him side-by-side as he campaigned for reelection. One day at a luncheon she was given a bouquet of roses. "They're beautiful," she told her husband. "But, I've got my hands full. I can carry them with my purse if you will carry our umbrella. I brought it because you never know about the weather."

Late in the afternoon, after they had made half a dozen stops with that many speeches plus a lot of handshaking, they got into their car to head for home. Suddenly, the Congressman's wife noticed that he was not carrying the umbrella.

"Where's my umbrella?" she demanded.

Looking a bit sheepish, he said, "I don't have any idea. I guess I put it down somewhere and forgot it."

"Well," she said, "One thing is for sure. If you weren't my husband, I wouldn't vote for you. It's terrible to think the important affairs of this country are in the hands of a man who can't even look after his wife's umbrella."

98.   The Congressman had a reputation for remembering

names and faces. He was pretty good at it, but he also faked a lot. Once when he was campaigning in his own city, his tailor was in the audience. After his speech, and when people were gathering around him to shake his hand, the tailor shook his hand and said in a quiet voice, "Remember me? I made your pants."

"Why certainly," the Congressman said, "I would have known you anywhere. My old friend, Major Pantz."

99.　The Congressman was addressing a group at a political rally and was quoting famous men right and left. "And as Daniel Webster says in his great unabridged dictionary . . ."

"Hold it," a voice in the audience called out, "Noah wrote the dictionary."

"I know what I'm talking about," the Congressman shouted. "Noah is the man who built the ark."

100.　The Congressman was facing opposition in his bid for reelection and he was conferring with his advertising consultant. "Don't you think the best thing for me to do is to stand on my record?"

"Not really," the expert said. "I think you should jump on your opponent's."

101.　After the Senator had made a stirring speech, a colleague said, "That was a great speech. I liked the positive and straightforward way that you skirted those issues."

298, 311, 357.

CONSERVATIVE

102.　All great peoples are conservative; slow to believe in novelties; patient of much error in actualities; deeply and forever certain of the greatness that is in law, in custom once solemnly established, and now long recognized as just and final.

–Thomas Carlyle

103.   We have a maxim in the House of Commons, and written on the walls of our house, that old ways are the safest and surest ways.

-Sir Edward Coke

104.   A conservative is a man who will not look at the new moon, out of respect for that "ancient institution," the old one.

-Douglas William Jerrold

105.   A conservative government is an organized hypocrisy.

-Benjamin Disraeli

CONSTITUTION

106.   We may be tossed upon an ocean where we can see no land—nor, perhaps, the sun or stars. But there is a chart and a compass for us to study, to consult, and to obey. That chart is the Constitution.

-Daniel Webster

107.   Constitutions should consist only of general provisions; the reason is that they must necessarily be permanent, and that they cannot calculate for the possible change of things.

-Alexander Hamilton

108.   The Constitution of the United States was made not merely for the generation that then existed, but for posterity— unlimited, undefined, endless, perpetual posterity.

-Henry Clay

109.   The time has come to take the Constitution down, to unroll it, to reread it, and to understand its provisions thoroughly.

-Andrew Johnson

CONTENTMENT

110.   In this world he who possesses a morsel of bread, and some nest in which to shelter himself, who is master or slave of no man, tell that man to live content; he possesses a very sweet existence.

–Omar Khayyám

CONVERSATION

111.   A single conversation across the table with a wise man is better than ten years' mere study of books.

–Henry Wadsworth Longfellow

402.

COURAGE

112.   The young man had been working at the lumber yard for only six weeks when he approached his boss for a raise.

"That's not the way to get promoted," the boss said. "You've got to work yourself up."

"I am worked up," the young fellow said, "can't you see I'm trembling all over."

113.   Courage is too often thought of in terms of heroism or dramatic action. But if you are observing, you may see the highest form of courage in the lives of everyday ordinary persons caught in a web of tragic circumstances.

–Author Unknown

50.

COURTESY

114.   A woman's car stalled when she stopped for a traffic light. No matter what she did, she couldn't get it started again.

The light had turned green, but there she sat, pushing the accelerator in and out and turning on the starter. Behind her an impatient man kept honking his horn—insistently.

Finally, the woman got out of her car and walked back to the man behind her who was making all the noise. "Excuse me," she said, "I can't seem to get my car to start. I wonder if you will help me. If you will get in my car and start it, I'll sit in your car and honk your horn for you."

358.

CRITICISM

115.   The 2nd grade teacher was taking her class on a field trip through the art museum. When they stopped in front of an abstract painting, one little girl said to the teacher, "What is that a picture of?"

"It's supposed to be two ladies having tea together," the teacher said.

"Well, why isn't it?" the little girl wanted to know.

35.

CURIOSITY

116.   Curiosity is one of the most permanent and certain characteristics of a vigorous intellect.

–Samuel Johnson

DANGER

117.   It is always darkest just before the day dawneth.

–Thomas Fuller

17, 75, 310.

DECISIONS

118. A lawyer was describing his troubles to a friend. "Think of it," he said. "In one day I have had three bothersome women for clients. One young lady wanted to get married, one married woman wanted a divorce, and an old maid didn't know what she wanted."

DEFIANCE

119. We have petitioned and our petitions have been disregarded; we have entreated and our entreaties have been scorned. We beg no more, we petition no longer, we now defy.

–William Jennings Bryan

DELAY

120. A commuter train that transported people back and forth from New Jersey to New York City was stranded in a snow storm one evening. The passengers who were returning home to New Jersey had to stay on the train in a snowdrift all night. By the middle of the next morning, a path had been cleared so that people could walk to a telephone.

One man called his office in New York and said, "I won't be at work today because I haven't gotten home from work yesterday."

121. Do not delay, the golden moments fly!

–Henry Wadsworth Longfellow

DISCIPLINE

122. The object of a liberal training is not learning, but discipline and the enlightenment of the mind.

–Woodrow Wilson

DISCUSSION

123.   Where the people rule, discussion is necessary.

–William Howard Taft

DISTURBANCE

124.   There was so much disturbance that the speaker couldn't be heard. He finally turned to the chairman and said, "I've been on my feet for over ten minutes and during that time there's been so much noise and interruptions that I can scarcely hear myself speak."

"Don't worry," came a voice, "you ain't missin' much."

DOCTOR

125.   A businessman had flown in to the city to "go through" one of the nation's most famous medical clinics. After three days of tests and consultation with several doctors, he was told that he was in good shape but that his blood pressure and cholesterol count were a bit too high.

He was happy with the verdict and took a taxi to the airport. The taxi driver was the kind who likes to talk, and he said to the man, "I picked you up at the clinic. Were you there to see a doctor."

"Yes," the man said, "I came for my annual checkup."

"Well," said the taxi driver, "you look like a healthy businessman except your blood pressure and cholesterol count are probably a bit too high."

204, 233, 352, 353, 356, 408.

ECONOMY

126.   A young fellow wrote home from college and said, "One of the subjects I'll be taking next semester is political economy."

His father wrote back and said, "Don't waste your time. That's a useless course to take. No successful politician ever economized—it just isn't done."

201, 345, 417.

EDUCATION

127. Education should not confine itself to books. It must train executive power, and try to create that right public opinion which is the most potent factor in the proper solution of all political and social questions. Book learning is very important, but it is by no means everything.

–Theodore Roosevelt

128. I consider a human soul without education like marble in a quarry, which shows none of its inherent beauties until the skill of the polisher sketches out the colors, makes the surface shine, and discovers every ornamental cloud, spot and vein that runs throughout the body of it.

–Joseph Addison

129. Every citizen is entitled to a liberal education . . . Despotism finds its chief support in ignorance. Knowledge and freedom go hand in hand.

–Calvin Coolidge

111, 122, 192, 193, 316.

ELECTION

130. What is the use of being elected or re-elected unless you stand for something?

–Grover Cleveland

41, 68, 306, 414, 425.

ENTHUSIASM

131.   The used car salesman was taking his prospect for a ride in a rather questionable car. Each time he would put it into gear, it would buck and jerk.

"What makes it jerk so whenever it starts up?" the prospect asked.

"Oh, that just shows how much enthusiasm it has. It's anxious to get going," the salesman said.

132.   A woman shopper went into a meat market and ordered two pounds of hamburger.

The clerk yelled at the butcher, "Two pounds of enthusiasm."

"Why do you call it enthusiasm?" the shopper asked.

"Because he puts everything he's got into it," the clerk said.

EQUALITY

133.   Fourscore and seven years ago our fathers brought forth on this continent a new nation, conceived in liberty, and dedicated to the proposition that all men are created equal.

–Abraham Lincoln

134.   There can be no truer principle than this—that every individual of the community at large has an equal right to the protection of government.

–Alexander Hamilton

135.   The only stable state is the one in which all men are equal before the law.

–Aristotle

386.

EXAGGERATION

136.	With customary newspaper exaggeration of army news we may be sure that in tomorrow's prints . . . all the little Colt revolvers will have grown into horse pistols.

EXCUSE

137.	The speaker was apologizing for being a few minutes late for the banquet. "I had to wait 20 minutes at the airport before I could get a taxi," he said. "Then we got into a terrible snarl of traffic. I finally said to the driver, 'For goodness sake, can't you go any faster?' "

And he said, "Yes, I can. But, I'm not allowed to leave my taxi."

120.

EXPERIENCE

138.	The personnel director was interviewing a job applicant. "You are asking for a rather high salary for a person with no experience in this kind of work."

"Yes, I guess that's right," the man said, "but the work will be much harder if I don't know anything about it."

139.	I have but one lamp by which my feet are guided, and that is the lamp of experience. I can tell nothing about the future save as I see it written by the finger of the past.

–Patrick Henry

140.	Experience is what you get while you are looking for something else.

10.

EXPERT

141.   The man who introduced me called me an expert. I'm reminded of the old definition of an expert, "Anyone who is 50 miles away from home with a briefcase in his hand." And my granddaughter says an expert "is like the bottom of a double boiler. It shoots off a lot of steam, but it never really knows what's cooking."

EXPLANATION

142.   A rather inebriated man was wandering aimlessly up and down the street at 2:00 a.m. Finally, after observing him for half an hour or so, a policeman stopped him and said, "What are you up to, walking up and down the streets at this hour of the morning? What's going on? I'd like to have an explanation."

        The man stared at the policeman with a hopeless look and said, "Shucks, officer, if I had an explanation, I'd go on home to my wife."

59, 87.

FAIRY TALE

143.   The little girl liked her father to read to her before she went to sleep at night. Her favorite story was "Snow White and The Seven Dwarfs." After reading the story over and over for several weeks, her father decided to put it on a tape recorder. Then one night he said to her, "Now, you don't need me here. All you have to do is to turn on the tape recorder."

        She tried it one night, but the next night she was tearful when she asked her father to read the story to her.

        "Can't you turn on the tape recorder?" he asked.

        "Yes," she said as she gave him a big hug, "but it can't hold me in its lap."

FAITH

144.   "This morning," the minister said, "I'm going to speak on the relationship between fact and faith. It is a fact that you are sitting here in the sanctuary. It also is a fact that I am standing here speaking. But it is faith that makes me believe that you might be listening to what I have to say."

145.   In the midst of a bad drought in Oklahoma, a minister called his congregation together to pray for rain. As he began the service, he looked out over the audience that was overflowing the church and said, "You all know why we are here. What I want to know is, why didn't any of you bring an umbrella?"

FAME

146.   A candidate who had been defeated in a close race checked into a motel in a nearby town shortly after the election. While he was registering, the desk clerk said, "Your face looks familiar. Haven't I seen you some place before?"

"You've probably seen my picture," the unlucky politician said, "it's been in all of the newspapers for the past three months."

"Come to think of it, I guess that's right," the man said. "I don't want to pry into your business, but why were the police hunting you?"

335.

FARMER

147.   A certain farmer's crops weren't flourishing and the County Agent had dropped by to help him and give him some constructive ideas. "Turnips are going to bring a good price this year, and you have some mighty good turnip land. What do you think of that?" the County Agent said.

"That sounds like a good idea," the farmer said, "but

even if I get the seed, my old woman's too blamed lazy to do the plowing and planting."

148.   And he gave it for his opinion . . . that whoever could make two ears of corn, or two blades of grass, to grow upon a spot of ground where only one grew before, would deserve better of mankind, and do more essential service to his country, than the whole race of politicians put together.

—Jonathan Swift

149.   "The agricultural population," says Cato, "produces the bravest men, the most valiant soldiers, and a class of citizens the least given of all to evil designs."

—Pliny The Elder

150.   Of all occupations from which gain is secured, there is none better than agriculture, nothing more productive, nothing sweeter, nothing more worthy of a free man.

—Cicero

325, 350.

FATHER

151.   A young married man rushed his wife to the hospital where she was due to have a baby. As she was being wheeled into the delivery room, the young husband took her by the hand and said, "Honey, are you sure you want to go through with this?"

5, 143.

FEAR

152.   A man who was making his first public speech was afraid that no one would applaud when he made an important point or would laugh when he told a funny story. To be sure that things went well, he invited a friend to come to the meeting and

help him. "When I take out my handkerchief and wipe my forehead," he said, "I want you to laugh. Then, when I pause and take a sip of water, I would like you to applaud."

"I'll be glad to be there," his friend said. "But, you had better switch those signals around, because I'll just naturally laugh out loud every time I see you taking a drink of water."

FISHING

153.   An airline pilot had a habit of staring intently out of the window toward the ground whenever he passed over a certain part of Kentucky on his Coast-to-Coast flights. One time his co-pilot said to him, "What's so interesting in this part of Kentucky? You always stare at it so hard when we pass over it?"

"I was raised down there," the pilot said. "I always look for that little creek that ran back of our house. When I was a boy, I used to sit there and fish. And I would always look at the airplanes going over and wish I were up there flying one of them. Now I look down and wish I were fishing."

FOOTBALL

154.   A man who was attending a football game was rather annoyed at a talkative fellow sitting next to him because the fellow kept a running commentary going about the game and all the players. Finally, the fellow said, "The reason I know so much about the game is that I played football in college. And for three years in a row, I helped Harvard beat Yale."

The first man turned to the talkative fellow, held out his hand and said, "Wonderful. Let's shake hands. I've always wanted to meet a man who attended Yale."

187.

FORCE

155.   There are two ways of contending, by law and by force: the first is proper to men; the second to beasts; but because

many times the first is insufficient, recourse must be had to the second.

-*Niccolo Machiavelli*

291.

FRANKNESS

156.   On an occasion of this kind it becomes more than a moral duty to speak one's mind. It becomes a pleasure.

-*Oscar Wilde*

157.   Be not ashamed to say what you are not ashamed to think.

-*Michel de Montaigne*

158.   If people would dare to speak to one another unreservedly there would be a good deal less sorrow in the world a hundred years hence.

-*Samuel Butler*

159.   Frankness invites frankness.

-*Ralph Waldo Emerson*

FREEDOM

160.   A Russian scientist was giving a lecture and was explaining how far Russia had advanced in the space age. "We already have put a space vehicle on the Moon," he said, "and within 20 years we'll be traveling to Mars and Jupiter and into outer space." As he ended his talk, he asked if there were any questions.

One man raised his hand and asked, "When will we be able to travel to London?"

161.   Posterity! You will never know how much it cost the present generation to preserve your freedom! I hope you will make good use of it! If you do not, I shall repent it in Heaven that I ever took half the pains to preserve it!

–John Adams

162.   Freedom of religion, freedom of the press, freedom of person under the protection of the habeas corpus; and trial by juries impartially selected,—these principles form the bright constellation which has gone before us.

–Thomas Jefferson

163.   History does not long entrust the care of freedom to the weak or the timid. We must acquire proficiency in defense and display stamina in purpose.

–Dwight D. Eisenhower

164.   Revolutions do not always establish freedom.

–Millard Fillmore

19, 46, 318, 319, 409.

FREEDOM OF SPEECH

165.   Freedom of speech means that even a donkey has a right to bray.

16.

FREE ENTERPRISE

166.   Agriculture, manufactures, commerce and navigation, the four pillars of our prosperity, are the most thriving when left most free to individual enterprise.

–Thomas Jefferson

FRIENDLINESS

167.   A young lady was given one of those little foreign cars for her graduation present. A friend said, "It looks mighty tiny. How many will it hold?"

"It's designed to hold four," she said, "but if everybody is well acquainted and friendly, I can get eight in it."

FUNERAL DIRECTOR

168.   The noted public speaker was in town to address the state convention of funeral directors. As he was finishing getting dressed for the banquet, he heard a knock on his hotel room door. When he opened it, a nicely dressed man standing there said, "I'm vice-president of the funeral directors association and I've come to escort you to the banquet. Are you about ready to go?"

"I'm all ready except for this tricky bow tie," the speaker said. "My wife usually comes with me and she always ties it. But this time I'm alone and I seem to be all thumbs when it comes to tying it."

"Oh, that's no problem," the funeral director said. "I can tie it for you. Just lie down on the floor."

GIVING

169.   The lavish banquet started with a fruit cup, followed with a bowl of cream of onion soup. Next came prime rib with a baked potato and asparagus tips and a peach Melba salad, hot rolls and butter. For dessert, the waiters paraded through the room with a display of flaming baked Alaska.

The speaker of the evening was making a plea for contributions to the Community Charity drive. He opened his speech by declaring, "Today, this is a bankrupt nation."

170.   We cannot exist without mutual help. All, therefore, that need aid have a right to ask it from their fellow men, and no one who has the power of granting can refuse it without guilt.

–Sir Walter Scott

GOAL

171.   A race horse doesn't worry about what people or the bettors think of him or of his performance. He just keeps his eyes fixed on the track and does his best.

384.

GOLF

172.   Not long ago a rather poor golfer sliced his tee shot and it went into the rough and landed on top of an anthill. For his second shot he used an iron. He missed his ball completely, and instead hit that anthill and scattered hundreds of ants in all direction. His second try was the same, and ants were sent flying every which way. As he lined up for his third try, one ant said to another, "Quick, if we're going to get out of this alive, we had better get on the ball."

GOSSIP

173.   The women's bridge club was always the scene of chitchat and gossip about this person and that. One afternoon the women were discussing a couple who had recently moved into the neighborhood. "They certainly do carry on something awful," one woman said. "They're scrapping and fighting every night. And they don't try to keep their voices down, either."

"I know who you are talking about," one of the other women said. "Their behavior is a disgrace."

"They're the talk of the neighborhood," a third woman said. "And some are on his side and some are on her side."

"And some of us," the fourth woman said, "are eccentric. We are minding our own business."

GOVERNMENT

174.   When once a man imbibes the principle that government was instituted to regulate all things, social and domestic, as well as political, it is the most natural error in the world that he should not stop where he began. He wants to apply it to every imaginable case of wrong . . . until there are no personal rights left to the people.

–Rutherford B. Hayes

175.   The spirit of resistance to government is so valuable on certain occasions, that I wish it to be always kept alive. It will often be exercised when wrong but better so than not to be exercised at all. I like a little rebellion now and then. It is like a storm in the atmosphere.

–Thomas Jefferson

176.   You cannot possibly have a broader basis for any government than that which includes all the people, with all their rights in their hands, and with an equal power to maintain their rights.

–William Lloyd Garrison

177.   A good government implies two things: fidelity to the object of government, which is the happiness of the people; secondly, a knowledge of the means by which that object can be best attained.

–James Madison

178.   I speak as one who believes the highest function of government is to give its citizens the security of peace, the opportunity to achieve, and the pursuit of happiness.

–Warren G. Harding

179.   A decent and manly examination of the acts of government should not only be tolerated, but encouraged.

–William Henry Harrison

180.   The less government we have, the better—the fewer laws, and the less confided power.

–Ralph Waldo Emerson

181.   Constructive government is not conducted on slogans—it is built on sound statesmanship.

–Herbert Hoover

182.   No man is good enough to govern another man without that other's consent.

–Abraham Lincoln

183.   What is the best government?
That which teaches us to govern ourselves.

–Johann Wolfgang Von Goethe

184.   I am one of those who do not believe that a national debt is a national blessing, but rather a curse to a republic; inasmuch as it is calculated to raise around the administration a moneyed aristocracy dangerous to the liberties of the country.

–Andrew Jackson

185.   Our country, which exhibits to the world the benefits of self-government, in developing all the sources of national prosperity owes to mankind the permanent example of a nation free from the blighting influence of a public debt.

–James K. Polk

46, 61, 96, 109, 280, 310, 333.

GRADUATION

186.   The young fellow brought home the worst report card you can imagine. The highest grade on it was a "D." His father studied it for a long time and then signed it with an "X."

"Why did you sign my report card like that?" the boy asked his father.

"Because," his father said, "with grades like you got, I don't want the teacher to think that you have a father who can read and write."

187.   The teacher had asked the students in the history class to list the people they thought were the eleven greatest Americans. After half an hour, everyone had turned in their lists except one boy.

The teacher said to him, "What's the matter? Can't you think of eleven great Americans?"

"I've got all but one of them," he said. "I haven't been able to decide on the quarterback."

188.   A boy and girl were standing there holding hands. One young lady who saw them whispered to her friend, "Look at them. Don't you think they are made for each other?"

Her friend said, "I certainly do. She's a headache and he's a pill."

189.   I'm here to speak to you who are graduating. Your parents and the other guests may listen if they like, but tonight I'll be talking to you. Because you are the most important people in this auditorium.

190.   You are the people who will be running this town, this state, this nation. Some of you will be the doctors, some the lawyers, and some of you will serve as our government officials.

191.   "Why do you hate school?" one student said to another.

"I don't hate school," his friend said, "I just hate the principle of the thing."

192.   You cannot teach a man anything; you can only help him to find it within himself.

–Galileo

193.   The roots of education are bitter, but the fruit is sweet.

–Aristotle

92, 122, 127, 129, 167, 171, 387, 420.

GRAMMAR

194.   The teacher was getting ready to give her students a test when one little fellow raised his hand. When the teacher asked him what he wanted he said, "I ain't got no pencil."

"I've told you a dozen times," the teacher said, "not to use that kind of language. Now listen carefully to me. 'I don't have a pencil. We don't have a pencil. You don't have a pencil. They don't have a pencil.' Now, do you understand?"

"You mean they ain't nobody got no pencils?" he said.

GREATNESS

195.   There is no such thing as a little country. The greatness of a people is no more determined by their number than the greatness of a man is determined by his height.

–Victor Hugo

320, 248, 251.

HAM

196.   I feel great today but three weeks ago I was seriously ill. I went to four different doctors but none of them could diagnose my problem. They had me scheduled for the hospital for observation and my wife was terribly worried about me.

Then she said she thought she could help me with an old family remedy. I figured anything was worth a try instead of the hospital, so she went to work on me. She fed me massive doses of sugar. I guess in two days I ate four or five pounds of sugar.

And suddenly, I was cured. I felt like a new man. No sign of sickness. I told her I thought she was wonderful. I told her I'd never heard of such a remedy and she said, "Oh, do you mean that you have never heard of a sugar-cured ham?"

HONOR

197.   That nation is worthless which does not joyfully stake everything in defense of her honor.

–Johann Christoph Friedrich Von Schiller

320.

HOTEL

198.   I am happy to be here tonight. This is a great hotel isn't it? This is the first time I've been here. When I checked in I was so impressed that I was afraid I wouldn't tip the bellman properly, so when he took my bags to my room, I just asked him. I said, "What is the average tip here?"

And he said, "Six dollars."

Well, I didn't want to look cheap, so I gave him the six dollars. But, I said to him, "If six dollars is the average tip here, and with all of the conventions that come here, you must be getting rich."

"No," he said, "all the time I've worked here, this is the first average I was ever able to get."

199.   The speaker was congratulating the hotel where the convention was being held. "I'm glad this isn't like the one where I stayed two weeks ago. The walls were so thin that I could hear everything going on next door. I finally got to sleep. But, in the middle of the night I was wakened by someone saying, 'Honey would you mind getting me a drink of water.' So, I went in the bathroom and got a glass of water and brought it back before I realized I was sleeping alone."

200.   The speaker for the big banquet was checking into the hotel. The desk clerk said, "Yes, we have a reservation for you but you didn't say what price room you want. Would you like one with a tub or a shower?"

"What's the difference?" the speaker asked.

"You have to stand up in the shower," the desk clerk said.

201.   The guest speaker was checking into the hotel and the desk clerk asked him, "Do you want the 85-dollars-a-day room or one for $95.00."

"What's the difference?" the speaker asked.

"In the $95.00 room," the desk clerk said, "you get free color television."

8.

HUNTING

202. I was speaking several weeks ago at an elementary school, and like today, I told the youngsters I would be willing to answer any questions they might have.

To get their attention, I told them about a recent hunting trip I had been on. I told them how I was awakened in the middle of the night with a roaring noise, and how I slipped out of my sleeping bag, and grabbed my gun and crawled out of my tent and shot a big bear in my pajamas.

When I asked if there were any questions, one little girl raised her hand and said, "I have a question. How did the bear get in your pajamas?"

HUSBAND

203. Two women were chatting. "How was the party that you and Bob went to last night?"

"Well," her friend said, "Bob was the life of the party. That ought to give you an idea of how dull it was."

262, 331, 334.

HYPOCHONDRIAC

204. A woman who was a hypochondriac had been pestering all of the local doctors for years. Nobody could please her. Then one day a new doctor moved to town. He had just graduated from medical school, and she was one of his first patients. "I have heart trouble," she told him. Then she spent about half an hour telling him about all of her symptoms. Finally she said. "I do have heart trouble, don't I?"

The young doctor said, "No, not necessarily. With the symptoms you have described to me, you may not have anything seriously wrong with you. It might not be anything more than gas on your stomach, and that should be easy to cure."

When he told her that, she jumped out of her chair and said, "Huh, you're nothing but a smart young whippersnapper.

Why, you're just out of school. You have a lot of nerve, disagreeing with an experienced invalid like me."

IDEA

205.   There is one thing stronger than all the armies in the world: an idea whose hour is come.

–Victor Hugo

89.

IDENTIFICATION

206.   A speaker looked over his audience before speaking and said, "Excuse me for taking that extra few seconds but I was looking to see if Mr. Pie was able to get to the meeting. As I got on the elevator in the lobby earlier today, there were half a dozen men and women on it. One man was wearing one of your convention badges. When the elevator stopped at the mezzanine floor an attractive young lady stepped in. Immediately she moved up close to this man and patted him on the cheek and said, 'Hi, Sweetie Pie.' And the lady standing next to him put out her hand to the young lady and said, 'I'm so glad to meet you—I'm Mrs. Pie.' "

207.   A man had a son named for him. One evening his wife answered the phone and a youngster's voice said, "Is George there?"

"Do you want little George or big George," she asked.

"I think I want big George," the youngster said, "you know, the one in the fourth grade."

IMPORTANCE

208.   A man had been called in to talk to the Internal Revenue Service about a serious discrepancy in his tax return. After much discussion and the usual questions by the taxpayer, the agent said, "Yes, I'm afraid you are right. We *do* plan to make a Federal case out of it."

INDECISION

209.   There is nothing in the world more pitiable than an irresolute man, oscillating between two feelings, who would willingly unite the two, and who does not perceive that nothing can unite them.

–Johann Wolfgang Von Goethe

INDEPENDENCE

210.   The owner of the company was conducting a sales meeting. He thought he would get the attention of his audience and put them at ease by telling a few funny stories. After each joke, everyone laughed uproariously—except one man sitting on the front row. He never cracked a smile. After the fourth or fifth joke, the boss looked at him and said, "What's the matter with you? Don't you have a sense of humor?"

"I don't have to laugh," the man said. "I'm quitting at the end of the week to take another job."

INDIANS

211.   A schoolgirl went to the public library and said to the librarian, "I want to learn something about the Seminole Indians for my school homework. I wonder if you can help me."

The librarian said she would be glad to help her. "You just sit over there at that table and I'll find what you want."

In about 15 minutes the librarian brought her a stack of books about two feet high and said, "There you are. That will tell you a lot about the Seminole Indians."

The little girl looked at the stack of books and said, "Thank you, but I didn't want to know that much about them."

255, 406.

INFLUENCE

212.   Any man who tries to excite class hatred, sectional hate, hate of creeds, any kind of hatred in our community, though he may affect to do it in the interest of the class he is addressing, is in the long run with absolute certainty that class's own worst enemy.

–Theodore Roosevelt

213. Everyone has an influence on public affairs if he will take the trouble to exert it.

–Calvin Coolidge

INNOCENCE

214. I hear much of people's calling out to punish the guilty, but very few are concerned to clear the innocent.

–Daniel Defoe

INTRODUCTION

215. Several weeks ago I was speaking to an oil dealer's convention in Pittsburgh. The man who introduced me had lost the introduction I had sent him and he didn't tell me that. He decided to make it up as he went along. In the end he introduced me as the man who had just made $800,000 in an oil deal in Texas. Of course, that wasn't exactly true. It wasn't an oil deal, it was a real estate deal. It wasn't in Texas, it was in Florida. Not only that, he got his figures mixed up. It wasn't $800,000, it was $800. Besides, that, it wasn't a profit, it was a loss.

216. [If the speakers ahead of you have touched the microphone, and fiddled around with it, you do the same—then use the following opener.]

I'm glad this thing is steady. The other night when I started to speak, the microphone dropped down. I pushed it up, but it dropped down again. After that had happened three or four times, the program chairman jumped up with a dime in his hand and began to tighten a set screw. As he worked on it, he said to the audience, "Don't worry, folks. Nothing's the matter except I think our speaker has a screw loose."

217. A Baltimore newspaperman was speaking before a group of cattle ranchers in a small Texas town. He was almost frightened to death when he noticed that most of the men in the audience were wearing six-shooters. His fears increased after he had finished speaking and sat down, because one of the men drew his guns and rushed toward the head table. "Don't be afraid of him," the chairman of the group said, "He's not going to bother you. He's after the man who introduced you."

218. Thank you for that kind introduction. I think the three hardest things in the world to do are these: first, trying to climb over a barbed-wire fence when it is leaning toward you. The second is trying to kiss a pretty girl when she is leaning away from you. The third is trying to live up to all of those nice things that Mr. Chairman has just said about me.

219. There is a service club in Spokane where they grade their speakers. A standing ovation rates four bells; an excellent speech wins three bells; an average speech will give you two bells. If you make a poor speech, you get one bell. They had one speaker who was awarded the no-bell prize.

220. The master of ceremonies at a big Chamber of Commerce dinner in Washington had enjoyed "one too many" at the preceding cocktail hour. When it came time to introduce the guest speaker, the Governor of the Virgin Islands, he said, "Ladies and Gentlemen, I now give you Virgin of Governor's Island."

221. Thank you, Mr. Chairman, for that gracious and flattering introduction. About the only thing you didn't say about me was that I was born in a log cabin. And you were right. I wasn't born in a log cabin. But my family did move into one as soon as they could afford it.

222. When the program chairman of the ladies' club luncheon introduced the speaker, she said, "We have only one speaker today. So, when he is finished speaking we can sit back and relax and enjoy ourselves because the rest of the program is going to be entertainment."

223.   Wow! After listening to all of those wonderful things that Mr. Chairman has just said, I know exactly how a waffle feels when somebody smothers it with honey.

224.   Thank you, Mr. Chairman, for that gracious introduction. You read it exactly as I wrote it.

225.   As the cow said to the farmer on a cold winter day, "Thanks for the warm hand."

226.   After that eloquent introduction, I can hardly wait to hear what I'm going to say.

23, 359, 368, 370, 372, 377.

JOGGING

227.   The man was telling a friend about a near accident. "I almost ran over a jogger this morning. I left home before daylight and as I turned a corner, there he was, right in front of my car. I had to act fast to swerve out of his way. Today you see them everywhere—mostly early in the morning. People think that jogging is something new. It's not. It was invented by a great-great-uncle of mine. He was a sergeant in the Confederate Army and he and two of his buddies started the custom during the battle of Vicksburg. Of course, when they caught them, they called it desertion."

JUDGE

228.   Thank you for that flattering introduction. It reminds me of a judge back home who was trying a divorce case. He had never had a case like this one. The woman had been married only one day. He was questioning her about her problem. "I can't understand why you want a divorce. You married the most eligible man in town. He was the best-looking man in town. He was rich. He didn't smoke. He didn't drink. All of your friends have been telling you those things about him for months and months. Then you married him yesterday and today you want a divorce. I can't understand it. What is your problem?"

"Well, judge. I guess that's my problem," the woman said. "That man was just naturally over-introduced."

KNOWLEDGE

229.   A man was chatting with a friend about his dog. "Your dog is smarter than mine," he said. "He knows all sorts of tricks. I can't teach my dog anything. How in the world do you do it?"

"Well," his friend said, "first, you have to be smarter than the dog."

129, 177, 301, 321, 338.

LABOR

230.   The laborer is the author of all greatness and wealth . . . With us, labor is regarded as highly respectable. When it is not so regarded, it is because man dishonors labor. We recognize that labor dishonors no man.

–Ulysses S. Grant

LATE

231.   Early one morning a man called for a taxi to take him to the airport. Half an hour later he called to say it had not arrived, and the dispatcher said it was on the way. After another half-hour he called again. "I need that taxi in a hurry," he said. "I've got to make that flight to the West Coast that is due to leave in 30 minutes."

The young lady at the taxi company said, "I'm sorry for the delay. But your cab should be there any minute now. But, don't worry. I'm sure you won't miss your plane because that flight is always late taking off."

"Well, one thing is for sure," the man said. "It will be late taking off this morning because I'm the pilot."

120, 137.

LAUGHTER

232.   A humorous speaker from Atlanta had made his first appearance in New England, where people are noted for their reticence and reserve. He felt that his speech had been a complete failure because nobody had laughed. He had told his funniest stories and most colorful anecdotes to no avail.

After the banquet, any number of people gathered around and shook his hand and told him how much they had enjoyed his presentation. As he was leaving the banquet hall, one little lady said to him, "You are the funniest speaker we ever heard. It was all we could do to keep from laughing."

152.

LAWYER

233.   A lawyer was talking to his son about his plans for college. "I'm hoping that you might study law," the man said. "Then you might work with me as a partner."

"I've thought about that," his son said, "but I've decided to be a doctor because doctors are more respected than lawyers."

"Where did you ever get that absurd idea?" his father asked.

"Well," his son said, "did you ever hear anybody cry out at a basketball game or a play, 'is there a lawyer in the house?' "

7, 118, 287.

LEADERSHIP

234.   It is better to have a lion at the head of an army of sheep, than a sheep at the head of an army of lions.

–Daniel Defoe

LEISURE

235.   We may divide the struggles of the human race into two chapters: first, the fight to get leisure; and second, what to do with our leisure when we have won it. Like all blessings, leisure is a bad thing unless it is well used.

-James A. Garfield

LIBERTY

236.   Is life so dear or peace so sweet as to be purchased at the price of chains and slavery? Forbid it, Almighty God! I know not what course others may take, but as for me, give me liberty, or give me death.

-Patrick Henry

237.   Those, who would give up essential liberty to purchase a little temporary safety, deserve neither liberty nor safety.

-Benjamin Franklin

49, 133, 160, 164, 154, 318, 319, 321.

LISTENING

238.   The little 6-year-old was visiting his grandmother, and somehow the conversation got around to the subject of spanking.

"My daddy doesn't spank me any more," the little fellow said.

"What does he do instead?" his grandmother asked.

"Oh," her little grandson said, "When I'm bad he just makes a speech about it."

"What does he say?" his grandmother wanted to know.

"I don't know," the little fellow said, "because I don't listen."

329, 341.

LITERATURE

239.   Life comes before literature, as the material always comes before the work. The hills are full of marble before the world blooms with statues.

–Phillips Brooks

LOGIC

240.   A third-grade teacher was trying to impress her students with the proper use of the verbs "lay" and "lie."

She asked the class, "At your house, what do they say? A hen lays or a hen lies?"

A little boy raised his hand and said, "At our house we lifts her up and takes a look."

LOVE

241.   A man had worked diligently for several years on his lawn. But no matter what he did or how hard he tried, every season his yard would be filled with dandelions. Finally, in desperation he wrote to his County Agent and asked, "What can I do with these dandelions?"

The reply that came back said, "Do what I have done. Learn to love them."

243, 248, 261, 390.

LOYALTY

242.   No personal consideration should stand in the way of performing a public duty.

–Ulysses S. Grant

MARRIAGE

243.   A college senior was sitting with his new girlfriend at a football game. As a substitute was put into the game and was trotting onto the field to take his place, the boy said to his girlfriend, "Take a good look at that fellow. I expect him to be our best man next year."

His girlfriend snuggled up against him and said, "That's the strangest way I ever heard of for a fellow to propose to a girl. But, regardless of how you said it, I accept. I know our marriage will be filled with nothing but happiness."

325, 344.

MAYOR

244.   A large crowd had gathered for the annual 4th of July barbecue. The announcer from the local radio station was acting as master of ceremonies for the day's events and the principal speaker was the mayor.

When it came time to introduce the mayor, the master of ceremonies said to the audience, "Remember, folks, right after the mayor finishes his speech, the high school band will play and call you all together again."

MEDICINE

245.   A woman took her dog to the veterinarian. He had been in a fight with a cat and was badly scratched up.

The doctor cleaned his wounds and patched him up and said, "He'll be all right. Just wash his scratched places in warm water about twice a day."

The woman seemed distraught over her pet and said, "Oh, but he's in such pain. Don't you think I should give him an aspirin, too?"

"Yes," the doctor said, "and take two yourself."

MEMORIAL

246.   American citizenship is a high estate. He who holds it is the peer of kings. It has been secured only by untold toil and effort. It will be maintained by no other method . . . To attempt to turn it into a thing of ease and inaction would be only to

debase it. To cease to struggle and toil and sacrifice for it is not only to cease to be worthy of it but is to start a retreat toward barbarism . . . This is the stand that those must maintain who are worthy to be called Americans.

–Calvin Coolidge

247.   Quiet and sincere sympathy is often the most welcome and efficient consolation to the afflicted. Said a wise man to one in deep sorrow, "I did not come to comfort you; God only can do that; but I did come to say how deeply and tenderly I feel for you in your affliction."

–Tryon Edwards

248.   Greatness is a spiritual condition worthy to excite love, interest, and admiration; and the outward proof of possessing greatness is, that we excite love, interest, and admiration.

–Matthew Arnold

249.   James Russell Lowell once wrote a eulogy of Louis Agassiz. His highest praise came when he said, "His magic was not far to seek—he was so human!"

250.   You cannot prevent the birds of sorrow from flying over your head, but you can prevent them from building nests in your hair.

–Persian Proverb

251.   Great men are meteors designed to burn so that the earth may be lighted.

–Napoleon Bonaparte

252.   A great life never dies. Great deeds are imperishable; great names immortal.

253.   The nation which forgets its defenders will be itself forgotten.

–Calvin Coolidge

254.   When good men die their goodness does not perish.

–Euripides

MEMORY

255.   A man and his wife were visiting Santa Fe, New Mexico. As they were strolling through the market where the Indians have all of their handicrafts displayed, they came to an old Indian who was sitting on his blanket being questioned by a dozen or so people who had gathered around.

"This old man has a 100 percent memory," someone said. "Ask him something. He remembers everything and everybody."

The man waited his turn and then said to the Indian, "What did you have for breakfast on November 27, 1942."

The Indian looked at him and said one word, "Eggs."

The man turned and said to his wife, "He's a fraud. Everybody eats eggs for breakfast. He's just being clever."

Four years later the man and his wife were back in Santa Fe. And there sat that same old Indian. Wanting to be friendly, the man rushed over to him, raised his right hand and said, "How!"

The Indian looked at him for a moment and said, "Over light."

98, 297, 311.

MICROPHONE

256.   [This opener works well if the speakers before you have had trouble with the microphone or otherwise had difficulty being heard.]

Can you all hear me? The other night I was speaking at a banquet, and right in the middle of my speech the public address system went dead. I tried to talk without it, but I noticed a fellow in the back with his hand up to his ear straining to hear me. He said "Louder." So, I raised my voice until I was shouting at him. Finally, I was yelling so loud that it bothered a man sitting down front. He couldn't stand it any more, so he jumped up and called out to the man in the back, "What's the matter back there, can't you hear him?"

"No, not a word," the man in the back shouted.

The man in front yelled back, "In that case, friend, move over. I'm coming back to sit with you."

216.

MINISTER

257.   The church board had voted to give the minister a lifetime contract. The announcement was made at a big family-night dinner in the church social hall. Everyone there cheered and clapped and assured the minister that they wanted him to stay as long as he lived.

Later, a friend said to the minister, "You didn't seem very excited about being given a lifetime contract. You ought to be the happiest man in town. Why, you are fixed for life."

"The reason I'm not too excited about it," the minister said, "is because I know another minister who was given a lifetime contract. Then several years later, after all of the old board members had retired and a new board was running things, they called him in, declared him dead, and fired him."

258.   The minister arrived at church one Sunday morning wearing a tiny patch on his face to cover up a cut. "This morning while I was shaving," he explained as he began his sermon, "I was thinking about my sermon and cut my face."

After church was over, he found a note slipped under the door of his study which read, "Next week while you're shaving, why don't you think about your face and cut your sermon?"

144.

MISTAKE

259.   The young man had been rushed to the emergency room at the hospital. He had a broken arm, and numerous cuts and bruises all over his body. "What in the world happened to you?" the doctor asked. "Were you in an automobile accident?"

"No," the young fellow said. "Nothing that serious."

"Well," asked the doctor, "what happened to you?"

"I was over at my new girlfriend's house and we were in the front room jitterbugging when her father came into the room. He is deaf and he couldn't hear the music from the stereo, so he threw me out the front door and into the street."

MIXED METAPHOR

260. The speaker was trying to make an impression on his audience. "If you don't stop shearing the wool off the sheep that lays the golden eggs," he shouted, "pretty soon, you will pump it dry."

MONEY

261. A man came home from work and found his wife crying. Having been married to her for more than 30 years, he was wise enough not to say anything to her. After he had taken off his hat and coat and mixed himself a drink and settled down in his chair to read the paper, she said to him, "You don't love me anymore. You come home and find me crying and you don't even ask me what's the matter."

He looked up at her and said, "I'm sorry, honey, but every time I ask you what's the matter, the answer ends up costing me money."

262. The woman was consulting a medium who was trying to reach her late departed husband for her. At last the medium said she was in contact with him and that the woman could speak to him directly.

Delighted, the woman said, "Tell me, Wilbur, if you didn't take it with you, where is it?"

263. Upon a good foundation a good building may be raised, and the best foundation in the world is money.

–Miguel de Cervantes Saavedra

48.

MOTHER

264.   The second-grade teacher had been giving her students a talk on science. She had explained about magnets and shown how they would pick up nails and other bits of iron. Then came the question period.

"My name begins with an "M," she said, "and I pick up things. What am I?"

A little boy on the front row said, "You're a mother."

265.   All I am, all I ever hope to be, I owe to my angel mother.

–Abraham Lincoln

266.   Did you ever hear of a great and good man who had not a good mother?

–John Adams

151, 330.

NATIONAL DEFENSE

267.   The national defense is one of the cardinal duties of a statesman.

–John Adams

NATURE

268.   Believe one who knows: you will find something greater in woods than in books. Trees and stones will teach you that which you can never learn from masters.

–St. Bernard of Clairvaux

269.   The study of Nature is intercourse with the Highest Mind. You should never trifle with Nature.

–Jean Louis Agassiz

270.   Let us permit nature to have her way; she understands her business better than we do.

–Michel De Montaigne

69.

NAVIGATION

271.   An ensign, who had graduated near the bottom of his class at Annapolis, was on his first cruise. The captain of the ship knew that the young man was particularly weak in navigation. Wishing to help him get some practical experience, he gave him the task of shooting the sun to determine the ship's position.

The ensign went to work with the sextant, and after awhile delivered his calculations to the captain.

Fifteen minutes later the captain called the ensign before him and said, "Let me see your ticket."

"Ticket?" the ensign asked. "I'm sorry but I don't understand. What ticket?"

"The ticket for the football game," the captain said. "Because according to your calculations, we're on the forty-yard line of the Rose Bowl."

NAVY

272.   A Navy, well organized, must constitute the natural and efficient defense of this country against all foreign hostility.

–John Adams

NEW IDEA

273.   An eight-year-old girl brought her report card home from school. She had several A's and a couple of B's, but the teacher had written across the bottom. "Betty is a smart little girl. But she has only one fault. She talks too much in school. I have a system I am going to try, which I think may break her of the habit."

Betty's father signed her report card and then wrote on the back, "please let me know if your system works on Betty because I would like to try it out on her mother."

NEWS

274.   The newsman on television had just told how happy Princess Diana was because she was going to have a baby. Little Alice, age eight, who was watching the news with the rest of the family, spoke up and said, "Mommy, how did Princess Diana know she was going to have a baby?"

Before her mother could answer, her younger brother blurted out, "She ought to know it. She watches the news on television, doesn't she?"

136.

NEWSPAPER

275.   An irate woman, waving a copy of a newspaper, rushed into the local newspaper office and said with a furious voice, "I want to see the editor of this rag. And I want to see him right now."

The clerk on the front desk said, "Do you wish to complain about something?

"Complain?" she shouted. "I could have done that with a letter. I came here in person to *revile* somebody."

317.

NEWSPAPERMAN

276.   An adventurous newspaper man had a reputation for trying anything once was invited to attend a fancy nudist party. Later he was telling a friend about it.

"Man, it was something," he said. "To begin with when I arrived at the house, the door was opened by the butler who was completely naked."

His friend interrupted him and said, "If he didn't have a butler's uniform on, how do you know he was the butler?"

"Well," said the newspaperman, "I knew one thing right away. It sure wasn't the maid."

378.

OPEN MIND

277. A woman was leaving her husband at home with the children as she headed for a big women's political rally.

"One thing you have to say for our organization," she explained to her husband, "is that all of us approach politics without bias or prejudice. Take me, for instance. I'm going to this meeting tonight with an open mind, even though I'm sure what I'll hear is nothing but political hogwash."

OPINION

278. Once when I spoke, a newspaperman was in the audience to write a report about it. This is what he said, "I do not want to appear to be biased with this report. But, the speaker was at a disadvantage. The sound system was turned up so loud I could hear him."

279. When I spoke to a convention banquet two weeks ago, a newspaperman was there to review it. You might say that I received mixed reactions. My wife liked my speech—but the reviewer didn't.

280. Free and unbiased exercise of political opinion is the only sure foundation and safeguard of republican government.

–Martin Van Buren

63, 93, 130, 301, 414.

OPPORTUNITY

281. One Sunday in a small tourist town, at the height of the season, a minister preached only five minutes. When he finished his sermon, he said, "I'm sorry to cut my sermon so short this morning but while I was eating breakfast our dog came into my

study and chewed up my sermon notes and left me with only one
page."

When the service was over and people were shaking
hands with the minister, one of the out-of-town visitors said to
him, "I was just wondering if that dog of yours has any pups. I'd
like to buy one from you and take it back home with me and give
it to our minister."

282.   Walter P. Chrysler said, "The reason so many people
never get anywhere in life is because when opportunity knocks,
they are out in the backyard looking for four-leaf clovers."

283.   A wise man will make more opportunities than he finds.

–Francis Bacon

324.

OPPOSITION

284.   People throw stones only at trees that have fruit on
them.

–Old Persian Proverb

PARKING

285.   The speaker said he was a wee bit nervous. "I'm parked
in front of a defective parking meter," he said. "I hope they don't
fix it before I finish my speech because I don't want a ticket.
When I parked, I noticed that the parking meter had a piece of
paper wrapped around it with a rubber band. It was a note. It
had two or three messages on it. One said, 'I put two quarters in
this meter.' and the person wrote his license number. The next
person had written the same thing. The next person said he had
put a quarter in, and he gave his license number. I left a note,
too. I put my license number on the same piece of paper, and
this is what I wrote, 'I'm not going to pay a quarter just to find
out if those other three fellows were lying.' "

38.

PATIENCE

286.   Day after day a senior citizen walked down to the recreation pier and sat and watched the people fish. He would bring his lunch and spend the day—just watching.

One day, a fellow who fished regularly said to the man, "You come down here every day and sit and watch the people fish. Don't you ever get the urge to do any fishing yourself?"

"I've often thought it might be fun," the man said, "but I don't really have the patience for it."

287.   A man went to see his lawyer and said to him, "I want to get a divorce. My wife hasn't spoken to me for three months."

The lawyer said to him, "If I were you, I'd think about that for a while. Don't be too hasty. Wives like that are mighty hard to find these days."

106, 114, 358.

PEACE

288.   We have for many years maintained with foreign governments the relations of honorable peace, and that such relations may be permanent is desired by every patriotic citizen of the Republic. But if we heed the teachings of history we shall not forget that in the life of every nation emergencies may arise when a resort to arms can alone save it from dishonor.

–Chester A. Arthur

289.   The name of peace is sweet and the thing itself good, but between peace and slavery there is the greatest difference.

–Cicero

290.   Peace, above all things, is to be desired, but blood must sometimes be spilled to obtain it on equable and lasting terms.

–Andrew Jackson

178, 236, 314.

PERSUASION

291.   A man was walking down a dark street one night on his way home when a drunk stepped out from behind a tree and pointed a gun at him. At the same time the drunk pulled a bottle of whiskey out of his pocket and handed it to the man, "Here," he said, "take a big drink of this or I'll shoot you."

The man was terrified and did as he was told. But after he had taken a swig of the whiskey he waid, "Wow! That's the worst stuff I ever tasted. I don't see how you can drink it."

"It's pretty hard to do," the drunk said. "That's why I stopped you. Now, you take the gun and force me to drink some."

PHYSICAL FITNESS

292.   We received a rude shock when during the War [WWI] we came to examine physically that "flower of American manhood." In the first draft over two and a half million men . . . the percentage of rejections on account of physical unfitness went . . . between twenty-five and thirty-three and a third percent . . . It means that one out of every three or four young Americans in their prime—between twenty-one and thirty—is unfit.

–Warren G. Harding

PLANNING

293.   I expect to spend the rest of my life in the future, so I want to be reasonably sure of what kind of future it's going to be. This is my reason for planning.

–Charles F. Kettering

281.

POINT OF VIEW

294. A fishing tackle salesman was chatting with a friend about his business. He was showing him some of the various lures that he sold to sporting goods stores. "This is our best seller for bass," he said, showing a brightly colored plug that was covered with stripes and spots.

"That sure is a bright-looking plug," the salesman's friend said. "But, I wouldn't think a bass would strike at such an outlandish looking thing."

"You may be right," the salesman said. "But this is our best seller. You see, we don't sell them to the fish. We sell them to the fishermen."

295. Recently during the question-and-answer period following his lecture, a listener asked a noted astronomer, "Do you think it is possible for the earth to be destroyed by a nuclear war?"

"So what?" the famous man said, "After all, the earth really isn't a major planet."

381.

POLITICAL PARTY

296. He serves his party best who serves the country best.

–Rutherford B. Hayes

POLITICIAN

297. The candidate had a poor memory for names and faces. But his wife was the opposite. She always went with her husband and stood at his elbow to tell him who people were as he approached them. But once at a cocktail party she became separated from him for a moment. Right then an attractive woman walked up to him. He was sure he knew her but he couldn't remember who she was. As he took her hand and smiled, a man pushed his way through the crowd toward him. Turning, he said to the man, "Well, look who's here, my old friend. Did your wife come with you?"

"You ought to know," the man said. "You're holding hands with her."

298.   A man who was running for Congress was speaking in a small town one night where most of his audience were going to vote for his opponent. Throughout his speech, people hissed and booed and otherwise showed their disapproval. When the meeting was over and most of the people had left, one old man came up to the candidate and said, "I wouldn't worry about the way people behaved this evening. The people who were here were the ignorant and stupid element in town. Everyone with any sense stayed at home."

299.   Two men were talking politics. "Who do you think was the greatest politician who ever lived?" the first one asked.

"Christopher Columbus," his friend replied instantly.

"I would have said George Washington," the first man said. "Why do you say Columbus?"

"Because," his friend said, "when he left Spain, his trip was government-financed. He didn't know where he was going. When he got to America, he didn't know where he was. And when he got back to Spain, he didn't know where he had been."

300.   A politician had so much trouble pronouncing words of more than two syllables that his secretary would spell them phonetically when she typed his speeches. That helped him a great deal. But he became so used to pronouncing everything syllable by syllable that once when he was speaking at a Fourth of July celebration, he said, "What this country needs is a return to the spirit of one-seven-seven-six."

301.   Two men were chatting on their way to the polls. One man said to his friend, "When it comes to the mayor's race, I don't want to vote for either of those men because I don't know them."

"I feel like you do," his friend said. "I don't want to vote for either one of them. But that's because I do know them."

302. After the Congressman had spoken at a political rally, he became involved in a hot argument with a man who criticized everything he had voted for. The Congressman began to get a bit riled up and said, "What do you take me for? Do you think I'm a fool?"

"No, I don't," the man said. "But of course, I could be wrong."

303. A politician had returned home one evening after making a speech and was telling his wife about it. "From the moment I was introduced," he said, "everyone in the audience sat there open-mouthed."

"Do you mean that everybody yawned at the same time?" his wife asked.

22, 66, 99, 100, 146, 311, 326, 362, 397.

POLITICS

304. The housewife had been active in politics for some time and finally, against her husband's wishes, she decided to run for office instead of merely helping others get elected. So, she filed for office and did all of the things that candidates do—held committee meetings, passed out literature, shook hands, kissed babies and made speeches.

One night she returned home from a political meeting, tired but jubilant. "At last," she said, "we've got things going my way. I'm sure we're going to sweep the county."

Her husband, crestfallen and sad, shook his head and said, "How about starting with your own living room?"

305. The daughter had gone off to college and was now in her senior year. During the past three years, she had developed certain political ideas that differed sharply from her father's. When her mother received word that her daughter was planning to come home for a visit, she wrote to her and said, "I'm so happy that you are coming home for a couple of weeks. But, to keep peace in the family, I wonder if you would put off your visit until after the election."

306.   A man was asked what he thought about the two candidates running for Circuit Judge.

"I know both of them," he said, "and I'm thankful that only one of them can get elected."

307.   We are apt to be deluded into false security by political catchwords, devised to flatter rather than instruct.

–James A. Garfield

67, 105, 126, 174, 179, 184, 185, 277, 309, 328, 374.

POPULARITY

308.   The man said to the taxi driver, "I want to go to a good place to eat. What about Johnny's Pizza Palace? I understand that is one of the best restaurants in town."

"People don't go there anymore," the taxi driver said. "It's too crowded."

POSTERITY

309.   The political candidate had been talking for more than an hour, and he did not seem to be anywhere near finished. As he waved his arms, he shouted, "And I want you to know that today I am speaking for posterity."

"You better hurry and finish," someone shouted from the rear, "or they'll be arriving soon to hear you."

104, 161.

POWER

310.   The dangers of a concentration of all power in the general government of a confederacy so vast as ours are too obvious to be disregarded.

–Franklin Pierce

52, 61, 180.

PRAYER

311.   A Congressman who had made a rather eloquent speech in the House, was being congratulated afterward by a colleague in the cloak room. "That was a touching speech you just made," he said to his friend. "I notice that you touched on religion and even quoted the Bible. I know you better than that. I'll bet you a five-dollar bill that you can't recite the Lord's Prayer—right now."

The first Congressman said, "That's a bet."

He then proceeded to say,

"Now I lay me down to sleep,
I pray the Lord my soul to keep,
If I should die before I wake,
I pray the Lord my soul to take."

The second Congressman reached in his wallet, took out a five-dollar bill and handed it to his friend. "You win," he said, "I didn't believe you could do it."

PREDICTION

312.   A man who had checked in for a flight at the airport purchased a $75,000 insurance policy from one of the automatic machines. Then, while he was waiting for his flight to be called, he stepped on one of those scales that gives you a fortune card with your weight stamped on it. His card read, "A recent investment is going to pay big dividends."

PREPARATION

313.   A cowboy had come into town and began to drink in the local saloon well before noon. By the middle of the afternoon he was drunk, and decided he had better head for the ranch. As he was walking down a back trail, he saw a rattlesnake coiled and ready to strike. "Go ahead and strike if you must," the cowboy said. "One thing for sure, I've never been better prepared."

314.   Preparation for war is the surest guaranty for

peace . . . Again and again we have owed peace to the fact that we were prepared for war.

–Theodore Roosevelt

PRESERVATION

315.   A man who was driving down a country road stopped at a farmer's roadside stand to buy some plums. "You have a beautiful place," he said to the farmer. "I'll bet you enjoy living out here where it is peaceful and quiet."

"Yes," the farmer said, "We like it out here. The only trouble is, I have to drive six miles into town to get a glass of whiskey."

"Why go to all that bother?" the man asked. "Why don't you buy a bottle and keep it in the house?"

"That sounds like a good idea," the farmer said, "but in my house whiskey don't keep."

PRESS

316.   Freedom of conscience, of education, of speech, of assembly are among the very fundamentals of democracy and all of them would be nullified should freedom of the press ever be successfully challenged.

–Franklin D. Roosevelt

317.   I find that it is absolutely useless to try to correct untruths or misrepresentations even of the most flagrant kind in the newspapers.

–Theodore Roosevelt

318.   The chief danger which threatens the influence and honor of the press is the tendency of its liberty to degenerate into license.

–James A. Garfield

319.   The freedom of the press is one of the great bulwarks of liberty, and can never be restrained but by despotic governments.

–Thomas Jefferson

320.   I would honor the man who would give to his country a good newspaper.

–Rutherford B. Hayes

321.   A diffusion of knowledge is the only guardian of true liberty.

–James Madison

136, 162.

PRETEND

322.   Do you believe in fairies? . . . If you believe, clap your hands!

–Sir James M. Barrie

PRICES

323.   A man walked up to the bar in a fancy restaurant and asked for a beer. When the bartender set it before him, he said, "That will be $1.50."

"What?" the man said. "$1.50 for a beer? I can get a beer for 50¢ in nearly any bar in town. Even the fanciest places only charge 75¢. What's this $1.50 for a beer?"

"It's the atmosphere," the bartender said. "For example look at the genuine oil paintings of pretty girls all around the walls. There's nothing like it in town."

The next afternoon the customer returned. He ordered a beer and put 75¢ on the counter and said, "I want a beer. And that's all I'm going to pay for it. I saw the pictures yesterday."

PRIVILEGE

324.   A young fellow was collecting for the Boys Club. A man gave him a $10.00 donation and the young fellow filled in a card for him. "Here is your membership card," he said. "You are now an honorary member of the Boys Club."

The man noticed that the honorary membership card gave him all the "rights and privileges" of membership. "What rights and privileges do I have?" he asked the boy.

The boy thought for a moment and then said, "I suppose that means you have the right and privilege of donating again next year."

PROMISE

325.   A young woman went to the police station and gave the desk sergeant a detailed description of a man she wanted them to find. She explained that the man had dragged her down two flights of stairs by her hair, choked her and threatened to beat her.

"With the description you have given us," the sergeant said, "we'll have him arrested and thrown in jail in no time at all."

"Oh," she said, "I don't want you to arrest him. I just want you to find him for me. He promised to marry me."

326.   A young lady was explaining why she had broken up with her boyfriend. "Everything was all right until he decided to run for political office. Before that, it was just me. But, now he's promising things to everybody."

PROPERTY

327.   Your own property is at stake when your neighbor's home is on fire.

–Horace

PSYCHIATRIST

328. Two psychiatrists had offices in the same building. One was a young man, new in the profession. The other was over 70 and had been practicing for 40-some years. Often at the end of their work day, they left the building at the same time. The young man always seemed to be utterly exhausted, but the older man never appeared to be the least bit tired.

"How do you do it?" the young man asked the other. "How can you look as fresh and relaxed and rested after listening all day to your patients complain and tell you their troubles."

"Who listens?" the wise old man asked.

PUBLIC DEBT

329. It is against sound policy and the genius of our institutions that a public debt should be permitted to exist a day longer than the means of the Treasury will enable the Government to pay it off.

-James K. Polk

QUAKER

330. A fourth-grade teacher in Pennsylvania gave her students the assignment of writing essays on the Quakers. One little girl wrote, "The Quakers are people who are quiet, meek, modest, and who never fight or talk back. My father is a Quaker. My mother is not."

QUIET

331. Dinner was over and the husband was reading the newspaper and his wife had settled into her chair to sew.

After a few minutes of silence, she looked up at him and said, "Darling, I have an idea. Why don't you read to me while I sew?"

He continued to read as he replied, "I have a better idea. Why don't you sew to me while I read?"

REAL ESTATE

332.   A little widow lady down in Florida was talked into a shady real estate deal by a fast-talking con artist. She lost $5,000 from her life's savings and went to the Better Business Bureau to file a complaint.

"On the face of it that was a risky deal," the man at the Bureau said. "Why didn't you investigate it before you invested your money. Didn't you know about the service we offer."

"Oh, yes," she said. "I knew about the Better Business Bureau, but I didn't come here first because I was afraid you'd tell me not to do it."

REBELLION

333.   A little rebellion, now and then, is a good thing, and as necessary in the political world as storms in the physical . . . It is a medicine necessary for the sound health of government.

–Thomas Jefferson

175.

RECOGNITION

334.   A charming young lady was exchanging chitchat with a woman who had arrived at a cocktail party a bit late. "These parties are so much fun," the young lady said to the stranger. "You never know what will happen. Here I am happily chatting with you, a nice lady I have never seen before. And a while ago, that man over there on the other side of the room was making a big fuss over me like getting my drink and asking me all about myself. Now, he won't even look this way."

"Maybe," said the lady she was chatting with, "it's because he saw me arrive. That's my husband."

335.   One time when the famous author received a letter addressed to "The World's Worst Novelist," he laughingly told a friend about it.

"Weren't you upset over such a letter?" his friend asked.

"Not really," the author said. "I have become hardened to people who criticize what I do. The only thing that bothered me was the fact that the postmaster knew where to send the letter."

146, 206.

REMEDY

336.   When something goes wrong, there is no need to ask who is to blame. The question should be, "What are we going to do to fix it?"

REPUTATION

337.   A couple had just returned home late at night from a dinner party. The wife said to her husband. "Well, as usual, you made a fool of yourself. I hope that nobody realized that you were sober."

RESEARCH

338.   The man met a young lady for the first time at a cocktail party. At his urging she later went to dinner with him and after that, dancing. When he took her home at 1:00 a.m. and was telling her good night, he asked her to marry him.

"That's mighty sudden," she said. "We only met a few hours ago. How do you know you want to marry me? You don't know anything about me."

"Oh, yes I do," he said. "I work in the computer department of the bank where your father has his bank account."

339.   I want you to know that my speech today has been carefully researched. I want to explain what that means. When someone steals material from one person, that is known as plagiarism. When he steals material from more than 15—that's research.

211.

RIGHT

340.   A taxi picked up a fare at the airport and drove him directly to his hotel. As the man got out of the cab, he read the meter and handed the taxi driver the exact change. "That's correct, isn't it?" he asked.

"Yes, that's correct," the taxi driver said, "but it isn't right!"

341.   The President hears a hundred voices telling him that he is the greatest man in the world. He must listen carefully indeed to hear the one voice that tells him he is not.

–Harry S. Truman

342.   I prefer to do right and get no thanks, rather than to do wrong and get no punishment.

–Cato the Elder

343.   Nothing is settled until it is settled right.

–Abraham Lincoln

ROMANCE

344.   Two Washington, D.C. secretaries were chatting, "I'll tell you the kind of man I'm looking for. I want one who will treat me as though I were a voter and he were a candidate."

SALESMANSHIP

345.   A young salesman had asked his girlfriend to marry him. She said she would be happy to, but he would have to ask her father for permission. "He's old-fashioned," she said, "and he might not say yes to the first man who asks him. I sure hope you can convince him."

The young salesman thought about that upcoming interview for a long time. Finally, when it came time to speak to the girl's father, he began the conversation by saying, "Sir, I have an idea that will save you a lot of money . . ."

346.   Two little boys were chatting. One had just received a puppy for his birthday and his little friend was complaining because his parents would not let him have one.

"You don't go about asking in the right way," the boy with the puppy said.

"I've begged and begged for a puppy," his friend said.

"That's where you are wrong," the first little boy said. "The best way to get a puppy is to beg for a baby brother and your folks will settle for a puppy. It works that way every time."

347.   A door-to-door salesman stepped up on the porch of a home in an attractive neighborhood to ring the doorbell. But, the door was open and he could see into the living room where a little boy was practicing on the piano.

Without knocking or ringing the bell, he said to the boy in a loud voice, "Is your mother home, young fellow?"

The kid looked at the salesman with a mean scowl and said, "What do you think?"

348.   The sales manager called all of his salesmen together for a special sales meeting. "Gentlemen," he said, "today, we're announcing a big sales contest. It will start tomorrow morning and will run for eight weeks."

His salesmen were excited, and one of the men on the front row asked, "What does the winner get?"

"What does he get?" the sales manager said. "He gets to keep his job."

25, 131, 294.

SIMPLICITY

349.   All great things are simple, and many can be expressed in a single word: freedom; justice; honor; duty; mercy; hope.

–Winston Churchill

SINCERITY

350.   A farmer drove across the country to see a man who had a cow for sale. "That looks like a healthy animal," the farmer said. "What sort of pedigree does it have?"

"Don't know," the man said.

"What about her butterfat production?" the farmer asked.

"Don't know," the man said.

"Do you know how many pounds of milk a year she gives?" the farmer asked.

"No, sir," the man said. "I really don't know all those things. But I do know this; she's an honest and sincere cow and she'll always do her best for you."

SLEEP

351.   I hope all of you are relaxed and comfortable—but not too comfortable. The other night I was speaking, and one man in the audience did get too comfortable and relaxed. He went to sleep. I don't mean he was nodding his head. This fellow went sound asleep. He moved the dishes out of the way and he really went to sleep. He embarrassed his wife. I saw her trying to kick him under the table, but she couldn't wake him. Finally, she picked up a spoon and tapped him on the head with it. That woke him up. He sat up and rubbed his head and said, "Honey, you're going to have to hit me harder than that. I can still hear him."

365.

SMOKING

352.   An elderly man who was in poor health went to the doctor for help. "There really isn't anything organically wrong with you," the doctor said. "You're just run down. Your body is tired. You are suffering from exhaustion. Drugs won't help you. What you need is a complete rest, away from your present environment. I recommend that you take a three-month trip around

the world by boat. Eat a lot of vegetables, go to bed early every night and take a nap during the middle of the day. And smoke only one cigar a day. I'm sure when you get back you'll feel like a new man."

The man did as he was told. And sure enough when he returned from the trip he felt great. His health was better than it had been in years.

He went to see his doctor and said, "Your advice certainly was exactly what I needed. I feel great. I've had only one problem, learning to smoke a cigar every day at my age was pretty hard to do."

353.   A man went to the doctor complaining about a pain in his foot. As soon as the doctor looked at it, he said, "You have a broken foot. When did it happen?"

"About a week ago," the man said.

"This is bad," the doctor said. "You could have had a serious problem letting it go without attention. Why did you wait so long to come see me?"

"Well," the man said, "every time I say something is wrong with me and that I am going to see a doctor, my wife says, 'See, I told you so. This time you'll *have* to stop smoking.' "

SPEAKER

354.   A man who had lived through the terrible Johnstown flood spent the rest of his life talking about his experience. He became so eloquent on the subject that he turned professional. After that, he went all over the country lecturing about it before huge crowds.

Eventually he died and went to Heaven. He had no sooner got settled when he began to pester St. Peter about giving one of his lectures. After a few days, St. Peter said to him. "It's all set. We've reserved an auditorium for you that will seat 4,000 and I'm sure every seat will be taken. But, there's one thing you should know—one person who will be in the audience will be a man named Noah."

355.   The speaker had attracted the attention of his audience by saying, "I'm going to illustrate the fact that nature is full of surprises by showing you something that you have never seen before. And I guarantee that you'll never see it again."

With those words he held up a peanut, shelled it and removed the inner part. "There you are," he said. "You never saw that before." Then he put it in his mouth, chewed it up and swallowed it and said, "And as I said, you're never going to see it again, either."

After his speech was over, one man shook his hand and said, "Your speech was interesting. I never knew I could learn so much from a nut."

356.   A prominent business man had been invited to make the keynote speech before 2,000 people at a statewide convention. This was the first time he had ever been invited to make a speech, and he was scared to death over the thought of it. As the fatal day approached he was almost a nervous wreck. Two days before the convention opened, he was rushed to the hospital with some sort of stomach disorder.

The doctors were not sure what his trouble was, so they decided to operate. As the surgeon cut into the man's stomach, a great swarm of butterflies flew out. Stunned, the surgeon said, "By George, he was right."

357.   The Congressman was invited to be the principal speaker at the big Fourth of July barbecue. When the local chairman wrote to him, he said, "We are delighted that you are going to speak to us at our big barbecue and Fourth of July celebration. The program will start with the mayor giving a word of welcome, then the American Legion drum and bugle corps will perform, then a high school student will read the Declaration of Independence, then your speech, and then the firing squad."

358.   The speaker was long-winded and dry. As he went on and on, people gradually slipped out until at last the audience had dwindled down to a single man in the front row.

"I wish to pause here, my friend," the speaker said to

this man, "to thank you for your courtesy in remaining to hear all of my speech."

"Oh, that's all right," the man said. "I don't need any thanks. I'm the next speaker."

359.   The chairman at the banquet introduced the speaker by saying, "I have been asked to introduce the speaker tonight. He is so distinguished that I could spend an hour telling you about him. And since I am not an experienced public speaker I am sure I would bore you to death. So, I'm not going to do it. Instead, I would like to introduce the man who is going to do that."

360.   A member of the Rotary Club had arrived at the meeting more than half an hour late and in the middle of the guest speaker's talk. As he tiptoed quietly to an empty seat, he said to the man next to him, "How long has the speaker been talking?"

"About 20 minutes," the other fellow said.

"What's he talking about?"

"I don't know. He hasn't said yet."

361.   Once when the master of ceremonies read a long introduction that listed at least two dozen activities and enterprises that the speaker had been involved in, a little lady on the front row leaned over to the person beside her and said, "My, you would have thought that such a distinguished-looking man would have been able to hold down a steady job, wouldn't you?"

362.   Two men had just finished listening to a political candidate give a long-winded and eloquent address well sprinkled with three syllable words.

"I think he uses all of those big words," one of the men said, "because he's afraid that if people knew what he was talking about, they would know that he didn't know what he was talking about."

363.   The inexperienced speaker stood up to speak, but was suddenly speechless. The huge audience dazed him. As he stammered and stuttered, a voice from the rear shouted. "Tell them all you know, Harry. It won't take very long."

Suddenly, his voice returned and he said loud and clear, "I'll tell them what we both know. It won't take any longer."

364.   During the early part of his talk, when the speaker was warming up his audience, he said. "I certainly hope my speech tonight comes out better than one I made last week. I had to stop right in the middle of it because of throat trouble—the program chairman threatened to cut it."

365.   The president of the service club was chatting with the speaker at the luncheon meeting.

"What is the hardest part of your work as a public speaker?" he asked.

"The hardest part of my work," the speaker said, "is waking up the audience after the man who introduces me has put them to sleep."

366.   The guest of honor had spoken on a technical subject and had read his speech verbatim. After the meeting was over he asked a friend what he thought of his presentation. "First, you read your speech," his friend said, "second, you didn't read it very well, and third, it wasn't worth reading."

367.   The speaker who had dreams of writing a book met a publisher one time and said, "I believe every successful public speaker has a good book in him."

"I'm sure that's true," the publisher said, "and I think that's where it should stay."

368.   When the program chairman for the women's club luncheon introduced the guest speaker, she said, "Ordinarily, the honor of presenting our guest speaker goes to our president. But today, I have been asked to do it because she is on her vacation down in Florida—and oh, how we all envy her."

369.   The long-winded speaker had been talking for more than an hour, except for a pause now and then to sip a hasty drink of water. When the meeting was over a fellow said to his friend, "That was the first time I ever saw a windmill run on water."

370.   I would like to begin by explaining our relationship. I'm your speaker. It is my job to talk to you. It is your job to listen. If you should finish before I do, you have my permission to take a nap.

371. The amazing thing about the human brain is that it begins to work the instant a person is born and never stops functioning until he stands up to make a speech.

372. There is an old proverb that says the only time a whale is in danger of being harpooned is when he rises to the surface and spouts off.

373. The eloquent man is he who is no beautiful speaker, but who is inwardly and desperately drunk with a certain belief.

–Ralph Waldo Emerson

374. "Did you hear my last speech?" a political candidate asked a friend.

"I certainly hope so," the friend said.

375. He that has no silver in his purse should have silver on his tongue.

–Thomas Fuller

376. The old proverb that says, "Blessed is he who has nothing to say and who refrains from saying it" does not apply to me tonight. I have something to say, and although I'll try to be brief, this is it:

377. Before I begin my speech, I have something I would like to say.

6, 23, 28, 33, 35, 137, 152, 168, 199, 206, 220, 222, 238, 285, 298, 300, 303, 309, 339, 379, 398, 400, 401.

STATISTICS

378. When people talk statistics, they always talk about averages. Average this, and average that. The thing to remember is that the average is exactly halfway between the best and the worst. It is the best of the worst and the worst of the best.

379. "It might interest you to know," the speaker said, "that every time I breathe, some person dies."

"Why don't you sterilize your mouth?" a voice in the rear cried out.

STOCK BROKER

380.   I'm honored to be here, of course. But, I don't know why I was invited to speak to a group of stockbrokers. Because, to tell you the truth, I don't know any more about how to make a sound investment in the stock market than you do.

STRANGER

381.   The young man timidly entered the room where his girlfriend's father was watching television. "Excuse me, sir," he said. "I have something rather serious I'd like to speak to you about. I hate to interrupt you, but this is real important."

The girl's father jumped up immediately and grabbed the young man by the hand and said, "I figured you were going to ask me. And the answer is yes. After all, my daughter's happiness comes first in this house. By all means, I give you my permission."

"Permission?" asked the young man. "Permission to do what?"

"To marry my daughter," the man said. "That's what you want to talk to me about isn't it?"

"No, sir," the young man said. "You see, I'm two payments behind on my motorcycle and unless I can get $320 dollars by Monday, they are going to repossess it. And I was wondering if you could lend me . . ."

"Absolutely not," the man said before the young man could finish his sentence. "You're a complete stranger. And I don't lend money to strangers."

SUCCESS

382.   Thank you for that vigorous round of applause. When I was introduced the other evening, nobody applauded. When I got home and told my wife about it, she said, "Then your speech must have been a failure."

And I told her, "No, the speech wasn't a failure, but the audience sure was."

383. The result proves the wisdom of the act.

–Ovid

384. To find his place and fill it is success for a man.

–Phillips Brooks

TAXES

385. No favored class should demand freedom from assessment, and the taxes should be so distributed as not to fall unduly on the poor, but rather on the accumulated wealth of the country.

–Andrew Johnson

386. The wisdom of man never yet contrived a system of taxation that would operate with perfect equality.

–Andrew Jackson

TEACHER

387. The little girl had misbehaved in school all week long. Every day she had been punished for some misdeed. Exasperated, the teacher said to her. "This is the fifth time I've had to punish you this week. What do you have to say about it?"

The little girl's answer was quick and to the point, "I'm glad it's Friday."

388. The sign in front of the school read, "School—Go Slow—Don't Kill a Child."

Underneath in a kid's hand print were the words, "Wait for a teacher."

389.   A mathematics professor who definitely was a male chauvinist was complaining to the dean about women being admitted into what had been an all-male college. "I will not have a girl in any of my classes," he said. "It's impossible to teach a boy calculus if there's a girl in the class."

"It can't possibly be that bad," the dean said. "There certainly must be an exception now and then."

"Well, if there is," the professor said, "he wouldn't be worth teaching."

TELEPHONE

390.   The man had installed a telephone answering unit to take messages when he was away from his office. Nearly every day when he would check it, he would hear a "click" which indicated that someone had called and did not leave a message. Then, once when he was in the office and had forgotten to turn it off, the mystery was solved. A recorded voice called in and began to talk about the merits of a new roofing material while his own recording was telling the caller how to leave a message. Both said at the same time, "Leave a message at the sound of the tone." Then complete silence.

Since nobody had answered his phone, it was counted as a "not in" call and the advertising voice continued to call back. And so, this non-conversation went on day after day.

Driving home that day, after making the discovery, he wondered if something was going on between the two robots—because his recording was in a man's voice while the call coming in was that of a charming sounding young lady.

391.   The man calling a business friend was surprised when a voice answered the telephone by saying, "Good afternoon, Murphy and McCree. Our automatic answering machine is in the shop being repaired. This is a live person speaking—may I help you?"

THANKSGIVING

392.   It has seemed to me fit and proper that [the gifts of God] should be solemnly, reverently, and gratefully acknowledged with one heart and one voice by the whole American people. I do, therefore, invite my fellow citizens . . . to set apart and observe the last Thursday of November next as a day of thanksgiving and praise to our beneficent Father who dwelleth in the heavens.

–Abraham Lincoln
Thanksgiving Proclamation, 1863

393. [Let us thank God] for His kind care and protection of the people of this country previous to their becoming a nation . . . for the great degree of tranquility, union and plenty which we have enjoyed . . . for the peaceable and rational manner in which we have been enabled to establish constitutions of government for our safety and happiness.

–George Washington
Thanksgiving Proclamation, 1789

394. Let us observe this day with reverence and with prayer that will rekindle in us the will and show us the way not only to preserve our blessings, but also to extend them to the four corners of the earth.

–John F. Kennedy
Thanksgiving Proclamation, 1961

395. Let all of us . . . give thanks to God and prayerful contemplation to those eternal truths and universal principles of Holy Scripture which have inspired such measure of true greatness as this nation has achieved.

–Dwight D. Eisenhower
Thanksgiving Proclamation, 1956

396. Let us . . . give thanks to God for His graciousness and generosity to us—pledge to Him our everlasting devotion—beseech His divine guidance and the wisdom and strength to recognize and follow that guidance.

–Lyndon B. Johnson
Thanksgiving Proclamation, 1964

THINK

397.   A political candidate was rushing to make a speech. As he pushed his way through the crowd, a long-time friend grabbed him by the elbow and said, "Hey, I haven't seen you in a long time. What do you think about the political situation today?"

"Please don't bother me right now," the candidate said. "I've got to start talking in about two minutes. This is no time to think."

TIMING

398.   The County Commissioner had been invited to speak to the students of the local elementary school on the subject of Americanism. "It's wonderful to live in America," he said. "I remember when I was a boy in grammar school, those were the happiest days of my life. And I can tell by looking into your faces that you, too, are happy. Why? Why are you so happy, today?"

Although he asked the question merely to make a point, he saw one little fellow on the front row raise his hand.

"Ah, young man," he said. "It looks as though you have an answer. Why are you so happy today?"

"Because," the kid said, "If you keep talking for another ten minutes, we won't have time for our history lesson and we'll go straight to recess."

399.   The luncheon speaker was explaining to his audience that he really didn't have time to cover his subject as thoroughly as he would like.

"The chairman of today's meeting said I could talk as long as I like," the speaker said, "but that after 1:30 there won't be anybody here but me."

400.   The lecturer was about to be introduced, when a news photographer was seen moving in close for a picture. The chairman, afraid that the speaker would be annoyed, whispered to the photographer and said, "Don't take his picture while he is speaking. Try to shoot him before he starts."

TOPIC

401. The speaker at the luncheon club had been introduced as a graduate of Yale. When he stood up to speak he announced that his topic would be "YALE." He began with the letter "Y" and said, "Y stands for youth." He talked for 15 minutes about youth. He then mentioned the letter "A". "That stands for achievement," he said. And he spoke for 15 minutes about achievement. Then he named the letter "L" and said it stood for loyalty, and he talked for 15 minutes on loyalty. Finally he came to the letter "E" which he said stood for enthusiasm. After he spoke for 20 minutes about the importance of enthusiasm, he finished his speech and sat down.

One listener was heard to say, "Thank goodness he didn't graduate from the Massachusetts Institute of Technology."

402. As a man arrived at a cocktail party, he was met at the door by the hostess who said, "I'm so glad you could come. First let me fix you a drink, then you can join the others. Those over by the lounge are discussing inflation, those by the mantle are talking about nuclear warfare, and those under the chandelier are deciding what should be done about our educational system. Take your pick."

78.

TOURIST

403. A woman who was traveling through the Holy Land was surprised when the tour guide told her group, "You will find that the roads all are excellent. We can travel in an air-conditioned bus all the way from Dan to Beersheba."

The woman leaned over and whispered to the person sitting next to her, "I never knew that Dan and Beersheba were places. I've heard about them all my life in the Bible but I thought they were husband and wife like Sodom and Gomorrah."

255.

TRADE

404.   The propensity to truck, barter, and exchange one thing for another . . . is common to all men, and is to be found in no other race of animals.

–Adam Smith

405.   No nation was ever ruined by trade.

–Benjamin Franklin

64, 89.

TRAVELER

406.   The man was telling about his trip to New Mexico.

"There I was," he said, "completely surrounded by Indians. Indians on my right, on my left, behind me and in front of me. It was horrible."

"My," gasped his friend, "what in the world did you do?"

"What *could* I do?" the man said. "I bought a blanket."

TRUTH

407.   A woman drove by an area where a crew of workmen were moving several large trees. As she drove past the crane that had a 40-foot pine tree in its grasp, something slipped and the tree crashed onto her car, causing several hundred dollars worth of damages.

Instantly, everyone rushed to help her. "We're glad you weren't injured," the foreman said. "And don't worry about your car. If it can't be repaired like new, the insurance company will buy you a new one."

"It's all right about the car," the woman said, "but somebody has got to go home with me and explain to my husband that the tree *hit me!*"

408.   A man said to his doctor, "I want you to give me a thorough examination and then tell me in plain words what's the matter with me. I don't want any of those fancy medical terms. Just tell me in plain language."

The doctor gave him a complete physical and then told him what he had found out. "There's nothing wrong with you," he said, "And you asked me for my diagnosis in simple language. This is it. You're lazy. Just plain lazy."

The man said to the doctor, "Now, if you don't mind, would you please give me the fancy medical term for it so I can tell my wife."

409.   The truth is found when men are free to pursue it.

–Franklin D. Roosevelt

115.

ULTIMATUM

410.   I hope we can reach an ultimatum here tonight. I feel like the farmer who went out to milk his cow one morning and said, "All right, Bessie, what will it be today? Milk or bar-becue?"

UNCERTAIN

411.   A young lady said to her roommate, "Where's your boyfriend this afternoon?"

"I'm not sure," she said. "If the ice is as thick as he thinks it is, he's skating. If it's as thin as I think it is, he's probably swimming."

UNDERSTANDING

412.   A Sunday school teacher who had a class of five-year-olds, opened the lesson by saying, "Today we are going to study about Peter. Can anybody tell me who Peter was?"

A little boy on the front row raised his hand.

"Oh, how nice," the teacher said. "Willy knows. Willy, please stand up and tell the class who Peter was."

Willy stood up and faced the class and said with great pride in his voice, "I fink he was a wabbit."

60, 105, 270.

VIRTUE

413.   The speaker was railing about the evils of drink. "I'll have you know that right here in this town there are 27 cocktail lounges, bars and taverns where whiskey is sold. And in the 50 years I have lived here, I have never been in one of them."

A rather sceptical and bored man in the back of the auditorium said in a loud voice, "Which one?"

VOTE

414.   A political poll taker had asked a woman how she had voted.

"Oh," the woman said, "I never vote. In no way do I want to feel a sense of guilt for what goes on in Washington."

415.   The ballot box is the surest arbiter of disputes among free men.

—James Buchanan

41, 68, 97.

WEAKNESS

416.   A man was sitting in the dentist's waiting room. The only other person waiting was an attractive young lady sitting opposite him. She was wearing a rather scant plaid skirt that kept creeping up above her knees. Every few minutes she would squirm a little and pull it down but almost at once it would creep up again. After one particular tussle with it, the man spoke to her in a fatherly voice and said, "Please don't bother trying to stretch that plaid skirt any more. You might as well know it, my weakness is whiskey."

WEDDING

417. A well dressed man entered a gunsmith's shop and said he wanted to buy a shotgun. The gunsmith saw that he was a man of some means so he showed him a fine English imported gun that was priced at $1,800.

"That's a beautiful gun," the man said, "but it's too expensive. I'd like to see something a little cheaper."

The gunsmith showed him other models, gradually going down in price. But, each time the man said it was more than he wanted to pay.

Finally, the gunsmith said, "Here is a mass-produced model. There isn't anything fancy about it. It sells for only $45.95."

"I'll take it," the man said. "That will do fine. Because, after all, it's only going to be a small wedding."

WILLINGNESS

418. A famous writer of romance novels received a letter from a young lady who had just graduated from journalism school. "I want to become a great writer and feel that working near you would help me. I would like a job as your secretary. In addition to that I would do anything else you might want me to do. And when I say anything, I mean *anything*."

A few days later she received a letter from the famous author's wife which read, "My husband already has a competent secretary, and I personally do everything else that needs to be done for him. And when I say everything, I mean *everything*."

419. A prominent member of the Governor's cabinet had just died, and an ambitious and obnoxious politician called on the Governor to ask that he be appointed to fill the man's unexpired term.

"I'd like to take his place," he told the Governor, "if it is all right with you."

"Oh," the Governor said, "it's all right with me if it's all right with the undertaker."

WISDOM

420.   Youth is the time to study wisdom; old age is the time to practice it.

–Rousseau

11, 283, 383.

WORK

421.   A tourist was traveling in the Appalachian Mountains and would stop from time to time to take pictures of the people and the scenery. He stopped in front of a small cottage where a man was sitting on the porch smoking a corncob pipe while his wife was working in a nearby garden. "That's pretty hard work for your wife, isn't it?"

"Yup," he said, "but she and me works in shifts."

"Oh," the tourist said, "when she gets tired, then you let her rest while you work in the garden. Is that right?"

"No, not like that," the mountaineer said, "what I mean is, when she gets tired working in the garden, then she shifts to the work in the kitchen."

13, 112.

Thematic Index for Openers

The numbers refer to the Openers listed in Chapter 4.

CHAPTER 5

Closers

NOW YOU ARE APPROACHING THE END OF YOUR SPEECH. How are you going to close it?

Are you going to say something that will "bring the curtain down" dramatically? Are you going to leave your audience hungering for more? Will you give them something to talk about afterwards? Will your closing remarks make them remember you?

Or are you going to stumble around like a drunk looking for an exit door in a dimly lighted barroom? Will you look at your watch, mumble something about your time running out, and sit down—like a soggy pancake hitting the floor?

Some speakers don't know when their speech is over and seem reluctant to step away from the lectern. How many times, following a speech, have you heard someone say, "He missed three or four good stopping-places"? Some people have even been known to say that about their minister's sermon on Sunday.

Did you ever hear a luncheon speaker say, "I think I have a few minutes left, do you have any questions?" Questions? If he had told his story fully there would be no unanswered questions.

A speech should be complete in itself. It should have an opening, a middle and an end. Nothing should be left out. You should not have to add anything when you've delivered it.

Think back in history to this scene for a moment. The date is March 23, 1775. The occasion, a meeting of the Virginia Convention in Richmond, Virginia. The speaker, Patrick Henry. This is the way he ended his speech—and made his name immortal: "I know not what course others may take; but as for me, give me liberty, or give me death!"

Can you imagine the effect on that group if he had said, "Now, before I sit down, are there any questions?"

Closing a speech is not easy. And most speakers run into trouble with those final few minutes. Yet what you say in that closing paragraph might put your name in the history books.

Let's face the truth. Everybody can't come up with a "Patrick Henry" ending. Even your most eloquent spellbinder is constantly on the lookout for ideas and material.

That's what this chapter is all about.

Here are 390 ways to end your speech. And like the openers in Chapter 4, some are humorous and some serious. And like an attention-getting opener, you must use your imagination and ingenuity to make your closing remarks fit *you* and your *audience*.

So, as we did at the beginning of Chapter 4, we'll start with the first story in this chapter, *#422*. This story will make an excellent closer for a luncheon speech where you have been informing your audience about something new or explaining how or why a certain community project is operating. It will *not* be effective if you have been speaking for some great cause and want to close by urging your audience to "storm the Bastille."

By changing a word or two here and there and adding a sentence, you can tell it like this, "Thank you for letting me join you for lunch today and for listening to me outline our plans for the Fall concert series. I have tried to stick to my subject and not wander too far off course. When I was a student at the university, we had an absent-minded professor who did that. He would start talking about some event in history and would end up giving us a lesson in botany.

"One evening he dropped in on his old friend, a doctor. They had a pleasant visit, including a game of chess. Before long a couple of hours had passed. As the professor was putting on his coat to leave, the doctor said, "The family's all well, I suppose?"

"Good heavens," the professor said, "That reminds me why I came to see you. My wife is lying in the middle of our living room floor having some sort of convulsion.

"Now, my wife isn't having a convulsion—I hope. And I do know why I came today. Again, thank you for listening."

That was a definite ending. There was no fumbling, no stumbling, no awkward hesitation. Not only that, there was nothing to be said after that.

But what about that speech where you want to stir people to action? How can you end that one?

Look at the next story, *#423*.

Suppose you have been talking for 20 or 30 minutes about a problem and have outlined a plan of action that you are urging your audience to follow. You "strike for the verdict" by saying something like this, "I know all of you agree that something must be done. I am sure that most of you think our plan is positive and that it will work. But, in order to make the plan work, we must work. With that in mind, I would leave you with this thought: Nowhere in the Bible do we find any reference to the *plans and objectives of the Apostles*. But you do find a whole book about The ACTS of the Apostles."

Let's take another look at that same speech. Maybe you have been giving an interim report on the United Way campaign. Maybe you are ahead of schedule and maybe you have been bragging about the good work everyone has been doing. But you want them to keep going and not let up during the next few days. So, you take the next story, *#424*, and use it like this: "In closing, I want to say again, you people have done an amazing job up to now. And I offer my most enthusiastic congratulations. But we still have to finish the job. We still have work to do. So, I would like you to leave this luncheon today remembering what Babe Ruth said once when he was congratulated on his great record. He said, 'Yesterday's home runs won't win today's ball game.' Thank you."

You might want to end your speech on a lighter vein and

yet get across the idea that your team must finish the job they have started so well. Look up the word "finish" and you find story *#539*. By using your imagination, you might close your speech this way: "Some years ago when Joe Louis retained his heavyweight title by knocking out Joe Walcott, he was later shown the picture of the fight. 'How did you like it?' he was asked.

"And Joe said, 'I think it had a real good ending.'

"And next week, when this great United Way campaign is finished, I hope you'll say the same thing—*it had a good ending*. And right now, I hope you'll say the same thing about my speech."

You always will be remembered if you can close your speech with a laugh. Thumb through this section of the book and you will come to story *#475*. This will get a big laugh if you tell it this way. "Before I close I want to thank you for inviting me here today. I want to thank you for your kind attention. You were a delightful audience. Of course, I knew you would be before I came. My wife asked me what sort of audience I thought I would have today and I told her it would be a sure thing. I told her she could bet on it.

"I had a friend who liked to bet on a sure thing. One day he went to the race track, and when it came time to put down his bet for the fifth race, there he was standing in line with a wad of money in his hand. There was a rather wealthy-looking man standing in front of him. The man turned to my friend and said, 'How are you betting?'

"My friend said, 'I'm betting $1,000 on Blue Belle. I figure I've got a sure thing.'

"The other man said, 'That's not a sure thing. There are six horses in that race and Blue Belle isn't the fastest horse. I ought to know, because I own Blue Belle.'

"My friend looked the man straight in the eye and said, 'I still think I've got a *sure thing*—because I own the other five.' "

And there's one *sure thing* about closing your speech— it's a do-it-yourself job. It's not like your introduction. The program chairman isn't going to stand up and say, "Our speaker will now end his speech." Putting together a closer takes more imagination and ingenuity and study than an opener—but the rewards are worth it.

So, with those examples behind you and a chapter full of lectern-tested closers ahead of you—good luck for many standing ovations!

The Closers

ABSENT MINDED

422.   Thank you for letting me speak to you today. I have tried to stick to my subject and not wander too far. When I was at the university we had an absent-minded professor who did that. One evening he dropped in on his old friend, a doctor. They had a pleasant visit, including a game of chess, and before long a couple of hours had passed. As the professor was putting on his coat to leave, the doctor said, "The family's all well, I suppose?"

"Good heavens," the professor said, "That reminds me why I came to see you. My wife is lying in the middle of our living room floor having some sort of convulsion."

649.

ACCOMPLISHMENT

423.   I have never heard anything about the plans and objectives of the Apostles. But, a whole book was written about "The Acts."

424.   Babe Ruth said, "Yesterday's home runs won't win today's ball game."

731.

ACCURACY

425.   The chief accountant said to his new assistant, a young lady just out of school, "We deal in figures here and we must be sure they are 100 percent accurate. So, before you bring me any reports to look at, be sure you add the figures at least five times."

The next day, the young lady brought him several pages of figures that she had been working on. "Here is the report you wanted," she said.

"Did you do as I said and add them up five times?" he asked.

"Oh, yes," she said, "and here are the five answers."

638, 742.

ACHIEVEMENT

426.   Destiny is not a matter of chance, it is a matter of choice; it is not a thing to be waited for, it is a thing to be achieved.

–William Jennings Bryan

427.   Unswerving loyalty to duty, constant devotion to truth, and a clear conscience will overcome every discouragement and surely lead the way to usefulness and high achievement.

–Grover Cleveland

428.   There is no rest for a messenger till the message is delivered.

–Joseph Conrad

432, 491, 522, 552, 571, 595, 608, 686, 689, 740.

ACTION

429.   Do all the good you can,
By all the means you can,
In all the ways you can,
In all the places you can,
At all the times you can,
To all the people you can,
As long as ever you can.

–John Wesley

430.   The man who goes alone can start today; but he who travels with another must wait till that other is ready.

–Henry David Thoreau

431.   Our grand business undoubtedly is, not to *see* what lies dimly at a distance, but to *do* what lies clearly at hand.

–Thomas Carlyle

432.   As for disappointing them, I should not so much mind; but I can't abide to disappoint myself.

–Oliver Goldsmith

433.   It is they who have the will to act who oftenest win the prizes.

–Xerxes

434.   The great end of life is not knowledge but action.

–T. H. Huxley

423, 491, 555, 577, 581, 598, 758.

ACTOR

435.   It was amateur night at the big dance hall. Often, some of the entertainers and producers from the television stations would catch the show to see if there were any promising stars to be discovered.

One night a young impersonator was doing his act when he noticed a famous movie star in the audience. He at once slipped an imitation of the visitor into his act. After the show was over, the amateur rushed up to the star and said, "You saw my act. You saw my imitation of you. What do you think?"

"Well," said the star, "all I can say is that one of us is pretty lousy."

ADVICE

436.   The fourth-grader was an "A" student in arithmetic but was the worst speller in the class. The teacher had him at the blackboard one day trying to teach him to spell. He was having difficulty with a word when one of his classmates blurted out, "Add an 'e' Joe."

In desperation, Joe said, "I'm not adding—I'm spelling."

AIM

437.   Too low they build who build beneath the stars.

–Edward Young

553, 554, 556.

AIRPLANE

438.   I want to thank you for listening this evening. My speech really isn't over, but I'm going to stop now because I have to catch a plane that takes off in exactly one hour.

AMBITION

439.   No bird soars too high if he soars with his own wings.

–William Blake

440.   Ambition is a commendable attribute, without which no man succeeds.

–Warren G. Harding

554, 556.

AMERICAN

441.   Please notice that the word "American" ends with "I can."

ANGER

442.   The greatest cure for anger is a good night's sleep.

679.

ANNIVERSARY

443.   Before I sit down, I want to say how much I have enjoyed sharing this delightful anniversary celebration. This will be an occasion I will long remember. I'll not be like a friend of mine who plays golf about three times a week. His wife was complaining about the amount of time he spent on the golf course. "You don't love me anymore," she said. "All you think about is playing golf. You don't even remember the date of our anniversary."

"I certainly do," he said. "I'll never forget it. That was the day after I shot an eagle on the fourth hole at Longwood Country Club."

444.   I want to say how happy I am to have been invited to speak on the occasion of the 36th anniversary of your great organization. This has been a delightful evening. It reminded me of the farmer's wife. She woke her husband up one morning and said, "Wake up. Today is our 36th wedding anniversary. I think we ought to celebrate. What do you say we kill a chicken?"

Her husband rolled over and said, "Why in the world do you want to punish a poor chicken for something that happened 36 years ago?"

649, 744.

APPLAUSE

445.   There's a modern proverb that says if you want to put a permanent finish on your car, you can do it by racing the train to the railroad crossing. And if you want to put a finish to my talk, all you have to do is start clapping.

ARBOR DAY

446.   I think that I shall never see
                 A poem lovely as a tree . . .
                 Poems are made by fools like me,
                 But only God can make a tree.

                                                    –Joyce Kilmer

447.　Woodman, spare that tree!
Touch not a single bough!
In youth it sheltered me,
And I'll protect it now.

　　　　　　　　　　　　　-George Pope Morris

ATTENTION

448.　The husband was watching the Saturday afternoon football game while his wife went shopping. When she came home, she found that the big pot of beans that was cooking on the stove had boiled over and the kitchen was a mess.

"What have you been doing while I was gone?" she shouted at her husband. "I told you to watch when the beans boiled over."

"I did," her husband said. "They boiled over at exactly 2:30."

729.

BABY-SITTER

449.　The man and his wife had been to a dinner party and when they returned home, the woman said to the babysitter, "Well, I hope little Wilbur was as good as gold while we were gone."

"No ma'am," the babysitter said. "He went off the gold standard about half an hour after you left."

635.

BALLOT

450.　The instrument of all reform in America is the ballot.

　　　　　　　　　　　　　-Woodrow Wilson

BEST

451.　Thank you for letting me speak to you today. I hope it was as good as a speech I made last week. Because after that one, when I had finished and sat down, everybody said it was the best thing I had ever done.

BOOKS

452.   People who *don't* read good books have no advantage over those who *can't* read them.

457.

BORING

453.   The host yawned, looked at his watch and said to his guests, "My, how time flies when you're talking to old friends. And who cares how late it is? Here it is already only twelve-fifteen and a half."

692, 698, 748, 799.

BREVITY

454.   The man saw a sign in the department store window, "Buy your girlfriend a bikini—it's the least you can do for her."

So, he bought her a bikini. Later he told his friend, "When you see a girl in one of those, the only thing left to the imagination is why they cost so much."

"Yes," his friend said, "a bikini sort of begins nowhere and stops all of a sudden."

BUILDING & LOAN

455.   The cocktail party was a huge success and all sorts of people were getting acquainted with each other. One fellow who thought he was the world's greatest gift to women was pestering a cute young lady. After a lot of chitchat and clever talk, he said, "Why don't you and I play Post Office?"

"If you want to play," she said. "I have a better idea. Why don't we play Building and Loan?"

"Building and Loan? he asked. "How do you play that?"
"It's easy," she said. "You get out of the building and leave me alone."

BUSINESS

456.   The chief business of America is business.

–Calvin Coolidge

CENSORSHIP

457.   Don't join the book burners. Don't think you're going to conceal faults by concealing evidence that they ever existed. Don't be afraid to go into your library and read every book, as long as any document does not offend our own ideas of decency. That should be our only censorship.

–Dwight D. Eisenhower

CHALLENGE

458.   Do not pray for easy lives. Pray to be stronger men. Do not pray for tasks equal to your powers. Pray for powers equal to your tasks.

–Phillips Brooks

CHANGE

459.   The speaker had finished his speech about the space program and was now in a question-and-answer period.

"What changes can we expect by the year 2,000?" someone asked.

"Well, one thing is certain," the speaker said, "Brigitte Bardot will be 65 years old."

713, 808.

CHARACTER

460.   In acquiring knowledge there is one thing equally important, and that is character. Nothing in the . . . world is worth so much, will last so long, and serve its possessor so well as good character.

–William McKinley

461.   It is not our nature to shirk our obligations. We have a heritage that constitutes the greatest resource of the nation. I call it the spirit and character of the American people.

–Harry S. Truman

462.   Lives of great men all remind us
                 We can make our lives sublime,
                 And departing, leave behind us
                 Footprints on the sands of time.

–Henry Wadsworth Longfellow

463.   When wealth is lost, nothing is lost;
                 When health is lost, something is lost;
                 When character is lost, all is lost!

464.   It is not a person's bank account, but his character, that determines whether or not he is rich or poor.

465.   People may doubt what you say. But one thing is certain; they will always believe what you do.

466.   It is better to be alone than in ill company.

–George Pettie

572, 578.

CIVILIZATION

467.   The true test of civilization is, not the census, nor the size of cities, nor the crops,—no, but the kind of man the country turns out.

–Ralph Waldo Emerson

468.   The cornerstone of modern civilization must continue to be religion and morality.

–William Howard Taft

543.

CLARITY

469.   The chicken farmer was losing a lot of his flock, and wrote to the Department of Agriculture in Washington. His letter read, "Gentlemen: Something is wrong with my chickens. Every morning when I come out, I find two or three of them lying on the ground cold and stiff with their feet in the air. Can you tell me what is the matter?"

About six weeks later he received a letter which said, "Dear Sir, Your chickens are dead."

COMMUNICATION

470.   The fourth-grade teacher was trying to instill the spirit of creativity in her students. "Today, I want you to write a composition without my giving you a subject to go by. I want this to show how you feel. Put down what's in you."

One little fellow turned in this essay, "In me there is a lot of blood, and a heart and a brain and a stomach. And in my stomach there is an apple, a peanut butter and jelly sandwich, and a glass of milk."

471.   A farmer had driven his team of mules into town to market. He was about two hours later than usual when he returned home. "What took you so long?" his wife wanted to know.

"Well," he said, "it was like this. On the way home I stopped and picked up the minister to give him a ride home. And after that those mules didn't understand a single word I said."

478.

COMPLIMENT

472.   It was a society function and the turnout was good. The speaker was an expert on ancient history. He spoke on the culture of the Medes and the Persians. After the speech was over, he was approached by an elegant lady who said:

"Your speech was most delightful. I found it especially interesting because, you see, my mother was a Meade."

451, 472, 531, 753.

COMPROMISE

473.   Half a loaf is better than no bread at all.

CONFIDENCE

474.   A man had purchased an old violin at a flea market. It had only one string, but that didn't seem to bother him. He would play on it hour after hour. Not only that, he always kept his finger in one spot. His wife put up with his noise for several weeks and finally she yelled at him and said, "If you are going to play on a violin, why don't you do like other people? Get one with four strings and then run your fingers up and down. That's the way the men in the symphony orchestra do."

"I know that's the way they play," her husband said. "I've watched them. All evening long they spend their time trying to find exactly the right note. Well, I've got news for you. I've found it."

475.   I had a friend who liked to bet on a sure thing. One day he went to the race track, and when it came time to put down his bet for the fifth race, there he was, standing in line with a wad of money in his hand. There was a rather wealthy-looking man standing in front of him. The man turned to my friend and said, "How are you betting?"

My friend said, "I'm betting $1,000 on Blue Belle. I figure I've got a sure thing."

The other man said, "That's not a sure thing. There are six horses in that race and Blue Belle isn't the fastest horse. I ought to know, because I own Blue Belle."

My friend looked the man straight in the eye and said, "I still think I've got a sure thing—because I own the other five."

487, 500, 505, 558, 587.

CONGRESSMAN

476.   A Congressman had just returned to Washington from his district where he had spent a week of intense campaigning. A fellow Member of Congress who had been trying to persuade him to change his views on a tax bill stopped him in the hall and said, "I've been reading about some of the things you said back in your district. I see where you have changed your views on that tax bill. I'm glad you finally saw the light."

"I didn't see the light," he replied. "I felt the heat."

477.   The Congressman had been out speaking all day and returned home late at night, tired and weary.

"How did your speeches go today?" his wife asked.

"All right, I guess," the Congressman said. "But I'm afraid some of the people in the audience didn't understand some of the things I was saying about our budget and fiscal policy."

"What makes you think that?" his wife asked.

"Because," he said, "I don't understand them myself."

478.   After the Congressman had spoken at a big campaign rally, one of his friends came up to him and said, "Mr. Congressman, after talking to those folks for nearly an hour, most of them still don't understand exactly where you stand on that question."

"Great," said the Congressman, "It took me four hours to write it that way."

701, 725.

CONSIDERATION

479.   The snow was coming down hard and the night was cold. The roads were slippery and the wind had dropped the wind-chill factor down to zero. Sir Lancelot, tired and weary, leaped from his horse and ran into a roadside stable.

"I am carrying an important message to King Arthur," he cried. "I need a fresh horse. Can you let me have a horse?"

"I am sorry," said the stableman, "all my horses are out. The only animal here is that big St. Bernard dog you see sleeping over there in the hay."

"Well," said Sir Lancelot, "He'll have to do. I'll take him until I can reach the next stable down the road."

"Oh, no!" begged the stableman, "I wouldn't want to put a knight out on a dog like this."

480.   A man who had a reputation for never getting home before two or three o'clock in the morning, went to see his doctor.

"It's about my wife, doctor," he said. "She suffers from insomnia so badly that sometimes she stays awake until after two in the morning. What can I do for her?"

The doctor said, "Start getting home earlier."

719.

CONSTITUTION

481.   The usefulness and permanency of this Government and the happiness of the millions over whom it spreads its protection will be best promoted by carefully abstaining from the exercise of all powers not clearly granted by the Constitution.

–James K. Polk

628, 694, 695.

CONTENTMENT

482.   With only plain rice to eat, with only water to drink, and with only an arm for a pillow, I am still content.

–Confucius

CONTRIBUTIONS

483.   When the speaker had finished his stirring speech for the local United Givers Fund, he said to his audience, "Now, as you make out your checks for the fund, please give in accordance with what you reported on your Form 1040."

CONVERSATION

484.   Two girls were roommates at college. One was vivacious and full of pep and the other was rather reserved and shy. The first girl often arranged dates for her friend but they usually turned into boring evenings. Trying to be helpful she said to her, "Look, I don't mind getting blind dates for you but when we go out together you should chat and join in the conversation more. If you need something to talk about why don't you read more. Read about famous people. That will give you something to chat about."

Her roommate did that, and several weeks later they went out on another date together. As usual, a lull developed in the conversation. So, remembering what her roommate had told her, the shy girl spoke up and said. "My wasn't it terrible what happened to the people on the Titanic?"

485.   The man was in the hospital being prepared for a gallbladder operation. As he was being wheeled into the operating room, he said to the doctor, "How long do you think my incision will be?"

"I'm not exactly sure at this point," the doctor said.

"Well, please do me a favor," the patient said. "Make it at least six inches long. My wife has a scar that is four inches long and her sister has one that is four-and-a-half inches long. And I want to have one longer than theirs so I won't have to listen to any more of their drivel and babble."

CONVICTION

486.   I can only say that I have acted upon my best convictions, without selfishness or malice, and by the help of God I shall continue to do so.

–Abraham Lincoln

504, 573.

COOPERATION

487.   By mutual confidence and mutual aid great deeds are done, and great discoveries made.

–Homer

COURAGE

488.   Courage is the best gift of all; courage stands before everything. It is what preserves our liberty, safety, life, and our homes and parents, our country and our children. Courage comprises all things; a man with courage has every blessing.

–Plautus

489.   It is better to live one day as a lion than a hundred years as a sheep.

–Old Persian Proverb

490.   Often the test of courage is not to die but to live.

–Vittorio Alfieri

524, 583.

CREDIT

491.   The world is divided into men and women who accomplish things and those who get all the credit.

731.

CRITICISM

492.   A man was telling a friend about a speech he had made recently.

"They liked my speech so much," he said, "that they gave me this gold watch. It's only the case. But, they said that if and when I ever come back, they would then give me the works."

609, 664.

DECISION

493.   The man who insists upon seeing with perfect clearness before he decides never decides.

–Henri Frederic Amiel

494.   A man cannot eat his cake and have it still.

–John Davies

654, 763.

DEMOCRACY

495.   As I would not be a *slave*, so I would not be a *master*. This expresses my idea of democracy. Whatever differs from this, to that extent of the difference, is no democracy.

–Abraham Lincoln

496.   No democracy can long survive which does not accept as fundamental to its very existence the recognition of the rights of its minorities.

–Franklin D. Roosevelt

497.   The Ship of Democracy, which has weathered all storms, may sink through the mutiny of those on board.

–Grover Cleveland

DETERMINATION

498.   Firmness of purpose is one of the most necessary sinews of character, and one of the best instruments of success.

Without it, genius wastes its efforts in a maze of inconsistencies.

–Lord Chesterfield

528, 606, 771.

DIFFERENCE

499.   A beggar was envious of the rich man who had just given him a dollar.

"You have no reason to envy me," the rich man said, "even if I do look prosperous. I have my troubles, too, you know."

"You're probably right," the beggar said. "You may have a lot of troubles but the difference is, I ain't got nothing else."

512.

DIFFICULTY

500.   Lack of confidence is not the result of difficulty; the difficulty comes from lack of confidence.

–Seneca

552, 586, 668.

DISCIPLINE

501.   When he asked why the younger generation shows such a lack of discipline, one father explained it this way: "The electric razor did away with the old-fashioned razor strop. The automatic furnace did away with the woodshed and the high interest rates made me lose my hair and the need for a hair brush. I guess the real reason I can't discipline the kids anymore is simple—I've just run out of weapons."

809.

DISGRACE

502.   A wise and good man can suffer no disgrace.

–Fabius Maximus

DIVORCE

503.   When a woman seeking a divorce came into court, the
Judge asked her age.
"I'm 79," she said.
"How old is your husband?" the judge asked.
"He's 82," she said.
"How long have you been married?" the judge asked.
"Sixty years," she said.
"After all of this time together," the judge asked, "why
do you want a divorce?"
And she said, "Enough's enough!"

DOUBTS

504.   Give me the benefit of your convictions, if you have
any, but keep your doubts to yourself, for I have enough of my
own.

–Johann Wolfgang von Goethe

505.   Doubt whom you will, but never doubt yourself.

–Christian Nestell Bovee

DRINKING

506.   The heavy drinker was handed his "first-today" drink
at a cocktail party by the host. Raising his own glass, the host
said, "What would you like to drink to?"
"If it's all right with you," the heavy drinker said, "I'd
like to drink to about 3 o'clock in the morning."

DUTY

507.   Duty, then, is the sublimest word in our language. Do
your duty in all things. You cannot do more. You should never
wish to do less.

–Robert E. Lee

427, 732.

EDUCATION

508.   How priceless is a liberal education! In itself what a rich
endowment! It is not impaired by age, but its value increases
with use. No one can employ it but its rightful owner. He alone
can illustrate its worth and enjoy its rewards. It cannot be inher-
ited or purchased. It must be acquired by individual effort. It
can be secured only by perseverance and self-denial. But it is as
free as the air we breathe . . . A liberal education is the prize of
individual industry. It is the greatest blessing that a man or
woman can enjoy, when supported by virtue, morality, and
noble aims.

–William McKinley

509.   Two women were chatting about their children. "What
plans does your son have—the one who is a freshman in college?
Is he going to become a doctor, or a lawyer or maybe a
preacher?"

"We aren't looking that far ahead," the boy's mother
said. "Right now we are wondering whether or not he'll become
a sophomore."

510.   The tax which will be paid for the purpose of education
is not more than the thousandth part of what will be paid to
kings, priests and nobles who will rise up among us if we leave
the people in ignorance.

–Thomas Jefferson

511.   Next in importance to freedom and justice is popular education, without which neither freedom nor justice can be permanently maintained.

–James A. Garfield

512. Education makes a greater difference between man and man than nature has made between man and brute.

–John Adams

513. The classroom—not the trench—is the frontier of freedom now and forevermore.

–Lyndon B. Johnson

514. The only thing more expensive than education is ignorance.

515. The money that is saved on education this year will be spent later on jails and reformatories.

516. The nation that has the schools has the future.

–Otto Von Bismarck

517. What greater or better gift can we offer the republic than to teach and instruct our youth?

–Cicero

518. The foundation of every state is the education of its youth.

–Diogenes Laertius

519. Public instruction should be the first object of government.

–Napoleon Bonaparte

572, 767, 809.

ENTHUSIASM

520. A salvage ship had been anchored over a wreck in the Bermuda Triangle and the deep-sea diver had been lowered to the ocean floor. He had hardly begun his work when an urgent message came over his telephone, "Come up. Come up. Hurry. The ship is sinking."

521.   Whatsoever thy hand findeth to do, do it with thy might.

–Ecclesiastes 9:10

522.   Nothing great was ever achieved without enthusiasm.

–Ralph Waldo Emerson

EQUALITY

523.   For he maketh his sun to rise on the evil and on the good, and sendeth rain on the just and on the unjust.

–Matthew 5:45

524.   In sport, in courage, and in the sight of heaven, all men meet on equal terms.

–Winston Churchill

EXAMPLE

525.   A man had just purchased a used car.
        "What model is it?" a friend asked.
        "It's not a model," the man said, "it's a horrible example."

EXCUSE

526.   The young fellow was late getting home from school. "I'm sorry I'm late," he said to his mother when he came in the door, "but the class is working on a science display for the county fair and I had to stay and put the finishing touches on the universe."

EXPERIENCE

527.   I have but one lamp by which my feet are guided, and that is the lamp of experience.

–Patrick Henry

807.

FAILURE

528.   They fail, and they alone, who have not striven.

–Thomas Bailey Aldrich

633.

FAINT

529.   The man passed out in a dead faint as he came out of his front door. The paramedics were called, and as they helped him regain consciousness, they asked if he knew what had caused him to faint.

"It was enough to make anybody faint," he said. "My son asked me for the keys to the garage, and instead of driving the car out, he came out with the lawn mower."

FAITH

530.   Men grow in stature only as they daily rededicate themselves to a noble faith.

–Dwight D. Eisenhower

732, 794.

FAME

531.   Two women stopped the famous lecturer and author in a theatre lobby one afternoon and said, "Don't you lecture?"

"Yes," said the famous man.

"Oh," said the first woman, "did you lecture yesterday morning at the public library?"

"Yes," he said.

"Oh, we thought we recognized you," said the woman. "We were there. Oh, you were simply won-der-ful, simply won-der-ful! What's your name?"

532.   A man looked up from his newspaper one evening and asked his wife, "Do you know how many really great men there are in this country?

"I don't know," said his wife, "but I do know there is one less than you think."

FAREWELL

533.   A man who had lost all of his money in a business deal and was flat broke, said to his girlfriend, "Darling, in spite of the fact that I'm not rich any more, will you still love me?"

"Certainly, honey," she said, "I'll love you always—even though I'll probably never see you again."

FARFETCHED

534.   I thank you for inviting me to be a part of your meeting. I want to thank you, too, for laughing at my efforts to tell a story or two. My wife told me the other night that all of my stories are farfetched. I asked her what she meant by farfetched and she said, "Because most of them were brought to this country on the *Mayflower*."

FIDELITY

535.   If I were to select a watchword that I would have every young man write above his door and on his heart, it would be that good word "fidelity."

–Benjamin Harrison

FIGHT

536.   There is a time to pray and a time to fight. This is the time to fight.

-*John Peter Gabriel Muhlenberg*

FINANCE

537.   The young bride went to the teller's window at the bank and said to the young lady, "Will you please show me how to make out a check so the money will come out of my husband's half of our joint checking account?"

538.   It is sheer madness to live in want in order to be wealthy when you die.

-*Juvenal*

439, 691.

FINISH

539.   When Joe Louis retained his heavyweight title by knocking out Joe Walcott, he was later shown the picture of the fight. "How did you like it?" he was asked.
     "I think it had a real good ending," Joe said.

639.

FIRE

540.   A rather drunk individual walked up to the hotel desk clerk about 1:00 a.m. and said, "I want to change rooms."
     "I can't understand why you want another room," the desk clerk said. "You have the best room in the hotel."
     "I don't care," the drunk said, "I've got to have another room if I'm going to get any sleep tonight."
     So the desk clerk transfered the man's registration to a

room on a lower floor and called the bellman and told him to help the man move. As the man and the bellman headed toward the elevator, the desk clerk out of curiosity said, "Excuse me, sir, do you mind telling me why you wanted to have your room changed?"

The drunk turned to him with a snarl and said, "Because the darn room is on fire."

FREEDOM

541.   In America, a glorious fire has been lighted upon the altar of liberty . . . Keep it burning, and let the sparks that continually go up from it fall on other altars, and light up in distant lands the fire of freedom.

–William Henry Harrison

542.   We have enjoyed so much freedom for so long that we are perhaps in danger of forgetting how much blood it cost to establish the Bill of Rights.

–Felix Frankfurter

543.   If a nation expects to be ignorant and free, in a state of civilization, it expects what never was and never will be.

–Thomas Jefferson

511, 513, 628.

FREEDOM OF THE PRESS

544.   When a thing ceases to be a subject of controversy, it ceases to be a subject of interest.

–William Hazlitt

545.   The very aim and end of our institutions is just this; that we may think what we like and say what we think.

–Rutherford B. Hayes

FUNERAL DIRECTOR

546. A motorist who had blocked the driveway to a funeral home when he parked his car, found this note under his windshield wiper when he returned. It was written on the letterhead of the funeral home and read, "Sorry to have to ask you, but will you please move your car. We hope to do business with you soon."

547. A man who had worked for a funeral director applied for a job as an insurance salesman. The personnel manager of the insurance firm asked him, "What did you like best about your former job."

The reply was quick and definite, "Working with people."

FUTURE

548. The future of this republic is in the hands of the American voter.

–Dwight D. Eisenhower

509, 585, 690, 691.

GENEROSITY

549. The chairman of the community fund drive was trying to get a rich banker to contribute. "You are the third man who has been here trying to get me to sign up," the banker said. "All of you know I am going to leave all my money to charity, so why keep after me each year?"

"Well," the chairman said. "I suppose it's like the pig and the cow who were talking about the same thing. The pig was complaining about the way he was treated. 'Nobody appreciates me,' he said. 'They are always telling you what lovely eyes you have and what a gentle nature you have. I know you give milk and cream, but look what we pigs give. We give bristles, and bacon, and ham, and people even pickle our feet. Besides that, they make the most expensive briefcases in the world out of pigskin. I don't see why you cows are so highly regarded.'

" 'Maybe,' said the cow, 'it's because we give while we are still alive.' "

GIRLFRIEND

550.   At this point I wonder if I'm not like the country boy who was walking through the woods with his girlfriend one Sunday afternoon. He put his arms around her and looked into her pretty blue eyes and said, "Honey, I love you more than anything in the world. Will you marry me?"

She didn't hesitate a second, "Oh, yes, I'll marry you."

They continued to walk through the woods and neither one of them said anything. After an hour of complete silence, the young lady couldn't stand it any longer and she turned to her boy friend and said, "Honey, why don't you say something?"

He looked again into her pretty blue eyes and said, "It seems to me that I've probably said too much as it is."

793.

GIVING

551.   Who gives himself with his alms feeds three—
Himself, his hungering neighbor, and me.

–James Russell Lowell
"The Vision of Sir Launfal"

483, 549.

GLORY

552.   The greater the difficulty, the greater the glory.

–Cicero

771.

GOALS

553.   I find the real thing in this world is not so much where we stand, as in what direction we are moving.

–Oliver Wendell Holmes

554.   He who attends to his greater self becomes a great man, and he who attends to his smaller self becomes a small man.

–Mencius

555.   To aim is not good enough; we must hit the target.

–Old Greek Proverb

556.   Hitch your wagon to a star.

–Ralph Waldo Emerson

428, 437, 462, 498, 662, 716.

GOODBYE

557.   A young man took his girlfriend to the county fair. After visiting many of the exhibits and enjoying some of the rides, they went to a sideshow where a magician was going to perform. The magician opened his show with a bit of patter that went like this: "Ladies and gentlemen, I am going to show you some amazing feats today. For one thing, I can see through anything. I can tell what you have in your pocket, I can read the dates on the coins in your pocket and the numbers on the bills in your wallet. I can see through wood, concrete, steel . . ."

Before he finished his little speech, the boy's girlfriend said to him. "Let's get out of here. This is no place for a girl wearing a cotton dress."

558.   The bank president was sensitive about his bald head and developed the habit of wearing his hat in the office. One day he was chatting with an old friend and said, "Sam, we've been friends in this town since we were boys. And when I became president of the bank, I thought you would open an account with us. But you never have. I've often wondered why?"

"Well, Harry," the man said, "I've come to the bank several times with that idea in mind, but whenever I do, I see you sitting there with your hat on and you always look like you are ready to get out of town at a moment's notice."

559.   I would like to close by saying "Carbolic Acid." I heard a speaker say that one time and afterward I asked him what he meant by it. And he said, "I always end my speeches that way. I used to say 'adios' which is goodbye in Spanish. And sometimes I'd say 'au revoir' which is goodbye in French. I even tried 'auf Wiedersehen.' That means goodbye in German. But, most people don't understand those languages. So, now I say 'Carbolic Acid.' That means goodbye in any language."

560.   A man had been visiting friends for dinner, and afterwards the conversation and chitchat dragged on and on until it was past time for him to leave. But finally he moved toward the door, still chatting away about this and that. Suddenly as he had his hand on the doorknob, he said, "There was something else I wanted to say, but for the moment it has slipped my mind."

"Maybe," said his host, "it was goodbye."

561.   As the speaker came to the end of his talk, he said, "The other day I saw a clever sign in the window of a travel agency. It said, 'Please Go Away.' And I think I'll follow their advice. Thanks for listening to me."

562.   A wife had been shopping and when she came home she showed her husband what she had bought. "This dress only cost me $64.00," she said. "Wasn't that a good buy?"

"Yes," her husband said, "goodbye, $64.00."

533.

GOSSIP

563.   The backyard gossip was talking to her next door neighbor. "I have just made a New Year's resolution," she said.

"During this year, I absolutely will not repeat gossip—so you have to listen carefully and catch it the first time I say it."

564.   A woman had been spreading a bit of gossip. When she finally stopped to get her breath, her friend asked her to tell her more.

"I can't tell you any more," she said, "because I've already told you more than I heard myself."

GOVERNMENT

565.   Governments do not make ideals, but ideals make governments. This is both historically and logically true.

-Calvin Coolidge

481, 519, 604, 612, 613, 625, 685, 696, 697, 702.

GRADUATION

566.   A member of the United States Cabinet was delivering the graduation speech at a university. It was well-written and was being delivered in a most inspiring manner. The theme was one of optimism and hope for the future.

Two foreign students were in the audience. One could understand English and the other could not.

"What is he saying," the second student said to the first.

"School is out," said the one who could understand English.

567.   Thank God every morning when you get up that you have something to do which must be done, whether you like it or not. Being forced to work, and forced to do your best, will breed in you temperance and self-control, diligence and strength of will, cheerfulness and content, and a hundred virtues which the idle never know.

-Charles Kingsley

568.   It is in the soil of ignorance that poverty is planted. It is in the soil of ignorance that disease flourishes. It is in the soil of ignorance that racial and religious strife takes root. It is in the soil of ignorance that Communism brings forth the bitter fruit of tyranny.

–Lyndon B. Johnson

569.   Before I finish my talk and sit down, I want to say one thing, I want to say it loud and clear. I'm betting on you. And when I say I'm betting on the young people of America, I want the world to know I'm betting on a sure thing. And nothing is better than betting on a sure thing.

570.   If a man can write a better book, preach a better sermon, or make a better mousetrap than his neighbor, though he builds his house in the woods, the world will make a beaten path to his door.

–Ralph Waldo Emerson

571.   Every man who can be a first-rate something—as every man can be who is a man at all—has no right to be a fifth-rate something; for a fifth-rate something is no better than a first-rate nothing.

–J. G. Holland

572.   Learn to know yourself to the end that you may improve your powers, your conduct, your character. This is the true aim of education and the best of all education is self-education.

–Rutherford B. Hayes

573.   Never give in! Never give in! Never, never, never. Never—in anything great or small, large or petty—never give in except to convictions of honor and good sense.

–Winston Churchill

574.   Each is given a bag of tools,
                           A shapeless mass,
                           A book of rules,

And each must make
Ere life has flown
A stumbling block
Or a stepping stone.

-R. L. Sharpe

575.   From this day on, please work harder than you ever
have before. Please do your best. Please do your job well.
Because the future is in your hands.

576.   It has always seemed to me that common sense is the
real solvent for the nation's problems at all times—common
sense and hard work.

-Calvin Coolidge

577.   Get action. Do things; be sane, don't fritter away your
time; create, act, take a place wherever you are and be somebody; get action.

-Theodore Roosevelt

578.   Friends, I am a thorough believer in the American test
of character. He will not build high who does not build for himself.

-Benjamin Harrison

579.   If you have great talents, industry will improve them; if
you have but modest abilities, industry will supply their
deficiencies.

-Sir Joshua Reynolds

580.   No person was ever honored for what he received.
Honor has been the reward for what he gave.

-Calvin Coolidge

581.   Think that day lost whose low descending sun
Views from thy hand no noble action done.

-Ancient proverb

582.   Wisdom is the principal thing; therefore get wisdom: and with all thy getting, get understanding.

–Proverbs 4:7

583.   Keep your fears to yourself, but share your courage with others.

–Robert Louis Stevenson

584.   A wise man will make more opportunities than he finds.

–Francis Bacon

585.   Hats off to the past; coats off to the future.

586.   Some men make difficulties. But, remember, difficulties make men.

587.   They can conquer who believe they can.

–John Dryden

437, 441, 460, 462, 466, 475, 488, 498, 500, 505, 508, 511, 543, 553, 554, 617, 704, 726, 727, 761, 810, 811.

GRANDCHILDREN

588.   Two women were chatting. "Have I ever shown you the pictures of my grandchildren?" the first asked.
        "No," her friend said, "and I certainly do appreciate it."

GRANDMOTHER

589.   The kindergarten teacher had been teaching the children to tell time. "Now when you get home, you can tell the time," she said. "I'm sure everyone has an alarm clock at home. Is there anyone who doesn't have an alarm clock?"
        One little girl raised her hand and said, "We don't need an alarm clock. We've got a grandmother."

590.   The little girl said, "Grandmother, were you ever a little girl?"

"Why, yes." Grandmother said, "I was a little girl just like you."

"Well, then," the little girl said, "I suppose you know how it feels to get an ice cream cone when you aren't expecting it."

591.   The little boy was visiting his grandmother. "Have you been a good little boy lately?" his grandmother asked. "Do you behave in church?"

"I think I do," he said. "Last Sunday the lady sitting behind us said she had never seen a little boy behave so."

GREATNESS

592.   It does not take great men to do great things, it only takes consecrated men.

–Phillips Brooks

HAPPINESS

593.   Here are seven rules for happiness. You follow the first six if you want to make a loved one happy. Just repeat one of these phrases: (1) I love you. (2) I'm going to take you out to dinner tonight. (3) All is forgiven. (4) Sleep until noon. (5) Keep the change. (6) Here is $20, spend it on yourself.

Rule number seven tells what to say to make your audience happy. (7) Thank you for inviting me to speak to you. My speech is over and I'm going to sit down.

594.   The Sunday school teacher said to her class, "It is our duty to make someone happy during the week. Have you done something to make someone happy?" she asked a little boy on the front row.

"Yes," he said without a moment's hesitation.

"That's fine. What did you do?" asked the teacher.

"I went to visit my Aunt Dorothy, and she was happy when I came home," he said.

595.   Happiness lies not in the mere possession of money; it lies in the joy of achievement, in the thrill of creative effort.

–Franklin D. Roosevelt

596.   If you count the sunny and cloudy days through a year, you will find that the sunshine predominates.

–Ovid

597.   Those who bring sunshine to the lives of others cannot keep it from themselves.

–Sir James M. Barrie

598.   Action may not always bring happiness; but there is no happiness without action.

–Benjamin Disraeli

616, 738.

HEART

599.   His heart was as great as the world, but there was no room in it to hold the memory of a wrong.

–Ralph Waldo Emerson

HOMESICK

600.   A mother received this letter from her little girl at camp:
    "Dear Mommy: I am having a wonderful time. I am not homesick. The food is good. The camp is good. The weather is good. The counseler is good. Love, Mary. P.S. When you come to visit me, please take me home."

HONOR

601.   An honorable defeat is better than a dishonorable victory.

–Millard Fillmore

580.

HUMILITY

602. Humility must always be the portion of any man who receives acclaim earned in the blood of his followers and the sacrifices of his friends.

–Dwight D. Eisenhower

IDEA

603. Ideas are the great warriors of the world, and a war that has no ideas behind it is simply brutality.

–James A. Garfield

IDEALS

604. Sometimes people call me an idealist. Well, that is the way I know I am an American. America is the only idealistic nation in the world.

–Woodrow Wilson

565, 619.

IGNORANCE

605. Ignorance and inconsideration are the two great causes of the ruin of mankind.

–John Adams

510, 514, 543, 568.

IMAGINATION

606. There are no limits to what we can do if we work together, except the limits to our own imagination and our determination to get the job done.

IMITATIONS

607.   After listening an hour to a guest at a cocktail party do bird imitations, his listeners were fit to scream.

"And now," he said, "I'll show you a real tough trick. You name a bird—any bird—just name any bird, and I'll imitate it."

"A homing pigeon," shouted one of the other guests.

INDIVIDUAL

608.   I am only one. But I am one.
                              I cannot do everything,
                                    but I can do something.
                              And by the grace of God,
                                    What I can do—I will do.

INSOMNIA

609.   After the speech, a man shook hands with the speaker and said he never had a more enjoyable evening.

"You found my remarks interesting, I trust," said the speaker.

"Not exactly," the man said, "but you sure did cure my insomnia."

480.

INSURANCE

610.   A man was seriously ill and in the hospital. Thinking he might not get well, and to while away the time, he began to work out how much his wife would be worth if and when he died. Later, when she was visiting him, he said, "I have figured out that my various insurance policies should give you about $52,000 when I die."

His wife said, "Now, Harry, you shouldn't talk like that. That's morbid. All I want is for you to get well." Then, after a few moments of silence, she said, "Did you figure in your GI insurance?"

JUDGMENT

611.   A good way to judge a man is to see which he would take if given a choice—a light load or a strong back.

807.

JUSTICE

612.   Justice is the end of government; and it is the end of society.

—James Madison

613.   The administration of justice is the firmest pillar of Government.

—George Washington

511, 674.

KNOWLEDGE

614.   The phone rang at eight o'clock in the morning in a small electronics plant at Cocoa Beach, Fla. The only person on the job at that time of the morning was the all-night guard. He picked up the phone and said, "Hello!"

"This is Major Knowit over at NASA," the voice on the line said. "I need some information in a hurry. What is the resistance rating and the total connected load of your model ARC-555-2627 unit?"

There was dead silence on the other end of the line.

"Hello, hello," the Major shouted, "don't you know anything about your electronic equipment?"

"Listen, Major," the night guard said, "when I picked up the phone and said 'Hello', I told you everything I know about electronics."

615.   Two young ladies were chatting. The first said to her friend, "So, the new lifeguard started teaching you to swim yesterday? What did you learn?"

Her friend said, "I learned that he's 27, single, and has a good job besides being a lifeguard."

616.   Knowledge is in every country the surest basis of public happiness.

–George Washington

434, 460, 788.

LABOR

617.   Remember that the genius of success is still the genius of labor. If hard work is not another name for talent, it is the best possible substitute for it . . . Go forth with brave, true hearts, knowing that fortune dwells in your brain and muscle.

–James A. Garfield

LARYNGITIS

618.   Now, I think I had better stop before I get hoarse. That's embarassing for a speaker. Three weeks ago I had laryngitis. It began rather mildly at the office in the morning, but by the time I was ready to go home I could hardly speak above a whisper. I thought it would be a good idea to stop at a doctor's office. A friend of mine told me about a good throat specialist who lived right on my way home. So, I stopped at his house and rang the doorbell. In about half a minute the door was opened by the doctor's wife. So, I whispered to her and said, "Is the doctor home?"

And she whispered back, "No, he's out of town. Come on in."

LAW

619.   We have never stopped sin by passing laws; and in the same way, we are not going to take a great moral ideal and achieve it merely by law.

–Dwight D. Eisenhower

620.   Liberty unregulated by law degenerates into anarchy, which soon becomes the most horrid of all despotism.

–Millard Fillmore

LEARNING

621.   There is no royal road to learning; no shortcut to the acquirement of any valuable art.

–Anthony Trollope

622.   As a field, however fertile, cannot be fruitful without cultivation, neither can a mind without learning.

–Cicero

LEAVE

623.   As the man was being wheeled into the operating room, the doctor looked down at him and said, "Before we operate, I think it is only fair that I tell you that only one person out of five ever recovers from this particular operation. Is there anything I can do for you before I operate?"

"Yes," the patient said, "help me put on my pants and shoes. I'm getting out of here before it's too late."

624.   Two little boys were playing with a wagon. Both of them were trying to get in it at the same time to coast down the hill. They weren't having much fun or enjoyment, and finally the little boy who owned the wagon said, "You know, one of us could have a lot more fun if you would get out of the wagon and go home."

660, 746, 754, 764.

LIBERTY

625.   Liberty has never come from the government. Liberty has always come from the subjects of it. The history of liberty is a history of resistance. The history of liberty is a history of limitations of governmental power, not the increase of it.

–Woodrow Wilson

626.   The tree of liberty must be refreshed from time to time with the blood of patriots and tyrants. It is its natural manure.

–Thomas Jefferson

627.   Eternal vigilance by the people is the price of liberty, and . . . you must pay the price if you wish to secure the blessing.

–Andrew Jackson

628.   A constitution of government, once changed from freedom, can never be restored. Liberty, once lost, is lost forever.

–John Adams

629.   God grants liberty only to those who love it, and are always ready to guard and defend it.

–Daniel Webster

630.   The tree of liberty grows only when watered by the blood of tyrants.

–Bertrand Barere

631.   Liberty without obedience is confusion, and obedience without liberty is slavery.

–William Penn

632.   The blessings of liberty are appreciated most when they have been lost.

488, 541, 542, 620, 673, 695, 702.

LIGHTHOUSE

633.   About a hundred years ago when the government was building a lighthouse on a rocky point in Alaska, a group of Indians used to sit all day and watch the men at work.

Finally it was completed and was dedicated with due ceremony. About a week later a terrible fog rolled in from the Pacific and the lighthouse got its first real workout. As usual, the Indians were on hand to see what would happen. After standing around for a while, one of them said, "White man stupid. Build big igloo. Light shine. Bell ding-dong. Horn go woo-woo. Fog come in same as always."

LIGHTNING

634.   "What are you doing hiding under the bed?" a mother asked her little girl.

"It's all that thunder and lightning," she said. "I don't want to get struck by lightning."

"Oh, that's silly," her mother said. "If lightning is going to strike you, it will strike you no matter where you are."

"That's all right," the little girl said, "but if it's going to strike me, I just want to be hard to find."

LITTLE GIRL

635.   A little girl's grouchy uncle had been left to baby-sit with her and put her to bed. His patience with children was nearly zero.

When she had gone to bed, and just before he turned out the light, she said, "Please tell me a bedtime story, Uncle Jim, "Please, please, please."

"Okay," he growled. "Once upon a time there was a little girl named Red Riding Hood and she met a wolf and the wolf ate up her grandmother. Now shut up and go to sleep."

636.   The little five-year-old was entertaining the guests while her mother was in the kitchen fixing tea and coffee for them. One of the visitors leaned over to the lady sitting next to her and said, "N-o-t v-e-r-y p-r-e-t-t-y is she?"

The little girl looked up at her with wide innocent eyes and said, "No, she isn't. But she sure is s-m-a-r-t."

590, 600, 634, 724, 766.

LOST

637.   A man and his wife who were avid backpackers, discovered during one of their hikes that they were lost. "I wonder where we went wrong?" the husband said.

"I don't know exactly," his wife said, "but if Emily Post were here she would say that somewhere along the way, we took the wrong fork."

LOVE

638.   The boss had just hired a new secretary, a cute young girl just out of school, and this was her first day on the job. The first letter he dictated to her was one to his wife who was out of town visiting her parents.

When the young lady brought the finished letter, neatly typed, for him to sign, he noticed that she had left off the sentimental ending, "I love you."

"Did you forget to put down the last sentence?" he asked.

"No, I didn't forget," she said. "I just didn't realize that you were still dictating the letter."

533, 667.

MAMMA BEAR

639.   We all know what Mamma Bear said about somebody eating her porridge. But, she also had this to say, "This is positively the last year I am going to serve as a den mother."

MARRIAGE

640.   A man was attending the wedding of a friend and was seated next to a rather talkative woman. While they were waiting for the ceremony to start she said to him, "Isn't this romantic. They've only known each other three weeks and now they are getting married."

"Well," he said, "That's one way of getting acquainted in a hurry."

641.   The young man had got up enough courage to ask his girlfriend's father for her hand in marriage.

"So," her father said, "you wish to become my son-in-law?"

"That wasn't the main idea," the young fellow said, "but I don't see any way out of it if I am going to marry your daughter."

MEMORIAL

642.   CROSSING THE BAR
     Sunset and evening star,
       And one clear call for me.
     And may there be no moaning of the bar,
       When I put out to sea.
     But such a tide as moving seems asleep
       Too full for sound and foam,
     When that which drew from out the
         boundless deep
     Turns again home.
     Twilight and evening bell.

and after that the dark!
And may there be no sadness of
farewell
When I embark.
For tho' from out our bourne of
Time and Place
The flood may bear me far,
I hope to see my Pilot face to face
When I have crossed the bar.

–Alfred Lord Tennyson

643.　　　　God of our fathers, known of old,
　　　　　　Lord of our far-flung battle-line,
　　　　　　Beneath whose awful Hand we hold
　　　　　　Dominion over palm and pine—
　　　　　　Lord God of Hosts, be with us yet,
　　　　　　Lest we forget—lest we forget!

–Rudyard Kipling

644.　　Horatio said of his friend Hamlet when he died. "His life was gentle and the elements so mixed in him that nature might stand on its feet and say to all the world—This was a man!"

645.　　Let us not lament too much the passing of our friends. They are not dead, but simply gone before us along the road which all must travel.

–Antiphanes

646.　　You might hear it said that a great life went out here. But great lives such as our departed friend's never go out. They go on!

647.　　To lose a friend is the greatest of all evils, but endeavour rather to rejoice that you possessed him than to mourn his loss.

–Seneca

648.   He was a man, take him for all in all, I shall not look upon his like again.

–William Shakespeare

MEMORY

649.   A woman was chatting with her neighbor and said, "Does your husband remember your wedding anniversary?"

"No he doesn't," said her neighbor. "So, I remind him of it in January and again in June. That way I always get two anniversary presents."

744.

MESSAGE

650.   A young man asked his uncle how he had become so rich. "It's a long story," said his uncle, "and while I am telling it we might as well save electricity." And he turned out the lights.

"No need to tell the story," said his nephew. "I got the message."

MISUNDERSTANDING

651.   A farmer went up to the barn to see how the new farmhand was doing. "Where is that horse I told you to take out and have shod?" he asked his new helper.

"Did you say 'shod'?" the new man asked with a look of astonishment. "I thought you said 'shot.' I've just finished burying her."

MOMENTUM

652.   The girl in the mailroom went to her boss and said, "The minister at our church is leaving, and this will be his last Sunday. I wonder if you would care to donate something. The congregation wants to give him a little momentum."

MOTHER

653.   The mother is the one supreme asset of national life; she is more important by far than the successful statesman, or businessman, or artist, or scientist.

–Theodore Roosevelt

MOTIVATION

654.   The famous paratrooper, who had made more than 200 jumps from a plane, was speaking to a group of young recruits. When he had finished his prepared talk and called for questions, one young fellow raised his hand and said, "What made you decide to make your first jump?"

The paratrooper's answer was quick and to the point, "An airplane at 20,000 feet with three dead engines."

MUSIC

655.   A man in the upstairs apartment yelled to the man downstairs, "If you don't stop playing that clarinet, I'll go crazy."

"Too late," the man yelled back at him. "I stopped an hour ago."

NATIONAL DEFENSE

656.   It is only by an effective militia that we can at once enjoy the repose of peace and bid defiance to foreign aggression; it is by the militia that we are constituted an armed nation, standing in perpetual panoply of defense in the presence of all the other nations of the earth.

–John Quincy Adams

657.   We must take care always to keep ourselves, by suitable establishments, in a respectable defensive posture.

–George Washington

NAVY

658.   A modern navy cannot be improvised. It must be built and in existence when the emergency arises.

–William Howard Taft

659.   A good navy is not a provocative of war. It is the surest guaranty of peace.

–Theodore Roosevelt

NEWLYWEDS

660.   The newlyweds had never had a quarrel, and they seemed to have the perfect marriage.

Then one morning at breakfast the young bride seemed upset and irritated at her husband.

"What's the matter, honey," he said. "Did I do something to upset you?"

"You certainly did," she replied with anger. "I dreamed last night that you were kissing another woman. And if I ever dream about it again, I'm going to pack up and leave you."

NEWSPAPER

661.   The newspaperman had been shipwrecked and was found by a tribe of cannibals and taken before their chief. "And what is your business?" the chief asked.

"I am a newspaperman," he said.

"An editor?" asked the chief.

"Not really an editor," the man said, "just a reporter."

"Well, I have a surprise for you," the chief said. "You are about to be promoted. After dinner tonight, you will be editor-in-chief."

OBSTACLES

662.   Problems and obstacles are those terrifying things that we see when we take our eyes off our goals.

668.

OLD MAN

663.   I hope I haven't taken up too much of your time today. I hope my speech wasn't like an old friend of mine who is 86. He's always dreamed of living to be a hundred years old. Last summer he went for his annual checkup and the doctor told him that he would have to give up drinking and smoking.

"And then will I live to be a hundred?" he asked the doctor.

"I can't guarantee that," the doctor said, "but it will sure seem like it."

OPINION

664.   A young speaker gave a special invitation to a highly regarded professor of public speaking to come and hear him give an after-dinner speech.

The professor came to the dinner, but slept through all of the young man's speech.

The young fellow was disappointed and upset and said to the professor, "How could you sleep when you knew how much I wanted your opinion?"

"Young man," the professor said, "sleep is an opinion."

665.   The mother of a talkative little girl always writes this note to her new teacher at the beginning of the school year: "The opinions expressed by this child are not necessarily those of her mother's side of the family."

666.   I never considered a difference of opinion in politics, in religion, in philosophy, as cause for withdrawing from a friend.

–Thomas Jefferson

486, 534, 699, 722, 780.

OPPORTUNITY

667.   Two friends were chatting. "How are you and that new girlfriend getting along—the one you wanted to marry? Did you propose to her yet?"

"Yes, but she turned me down," the other fellow said.

"What? Turned you down?" his friend said. "You didn't impress her enough. Why didn't you tell her about your 90-year-old millionaire uncle?"

"I did," the other fellow said. "Now, she's my new rich aunt."

668.   The block of granite which was an obstacle in the pathway of the weak becomes a stepping-stone in the pathway of the strong.

–Thomas Carlyle

669.   I gather the rose from the thorn, the gold from the earth, the pearl from the oyster.

–St. Jerome

670.   As we have therefore opportunity, let us do good unto all men.

–Galatians 6:10

671.   Small opportunities are often the beginning of great enterprises.

–Demosthenes

574, 584.

OPTIMISM

672.   The man came to the breakfast table with a downcast look. It was obvious that he hated the thought of going to work. His wife, in an effort to cheer him up said, "Look at it this way. In only 16 hours you'll be able to go back to bed."

566, 669.

ORDER

673.   Order means light and peace, inward liberty and free command over oneself; order is power.

–Henri-Frederic Amiel

PACIFISM

674.   Professional pacifists should be regarded as traitors to the great cause of justice and humanity.

–Theodore Roosevelt

PARKING

675.   A man noticed a young lady edging her car back and forth in a tight parking space. Being a helpful fellow, he stopped to help her. He signaled how she should turn the wheel and when to go forward and when to back. After a few minutes, under his expert directing, the car was nestled tightly against the curb.

"There you are," he said. "Snug as a bug in a rug."

"I know," she said, "and I appreciate your help. But, I wasn't trying to park it. I was trying to get out."

546.

PATIENCE

676.   No great thing is created suddenly, any more than a bunch of grapes or a fig. If you tell me that you desire a fig, I answer you that there must be time. Let it first blossom, then bear fruit, then ripen.

–Epictetus

677.   It has been my observation in life that, if one will only exercise patience to wait, his wants are likely to be filled.

–Calvin Coolidge

678.   There is a limit at which forbearance ceases to be a virtue.

–Edmund Burke

679.   Beware the fury of a patient man.

–John Dryden

442, 687, 799, 800, 801.

PATRIOTISM

680. Patriotism is easy to understand in America. It means looking out for yourself by looking out for your country.

–Calvin Coolidge

PAYMENT

681. After a well known speaker had entertained a civic club at a banquet in his home town, the chairman gave him a small honorarium. Knowing that even that small amount was a burden on the club, he returned the check and said, "I was happy to donate my time. Please put this money to a good cause with my compliments."

"Thank you very much," the chairman said. "We'll put this in our special fund."

Curious, the speaker said, "What's the special fund used for?"

"Oh," the chairman said, "it's a fund we have set up so we can pay for better speakers from now on."

792.

PEACE

682. They shall beat their swords into ploughshares, and their spears into pruning hooks; nation shall not lift up sword against nation, neither shall they learn war any more.

–Isaiah 2:4

683. To be prepared for war is one of the most effective means of preserving peace.

–George Washington

684. To maintain peace in the future it is necessary to be prepared for war.

–Ulysses S. Grant

656, 659, 673, 707, 708.

PEOPLE

685.   Our Government springs from and was made for the people—not the people for the Government. To them it owes an allegiance; from them it must derive its courage, strength, and wisdom.

–Andrew Johnson

547.

PERSEVERANCE

686.   Great works are performed not by strength but by perseverance.

–Samuel Johnson

687.   Perseverance is more prevailing than violence.

–Plutarch

PERSISTENCE

688.   A hen keeps on digging worms and laying eggs, regardless of "conditions." If the ground is hard, she scratches harder. If it is dry, she digs deeper. If she strikes rock, she works around it. But always she digs up worms and turns them into hard-shelled profits. She saves her breath for digging and her cackle for eggs.

–Author Unknown

689.   Today's mighty oak is just yesterday's little acorn that held its ground.

428.

PLANNING

690.   A businessman would stop his car each morning on the way to his office as he passed the state mental institution. He would pull off of the road and watch one of the inmates who was always practicing baseball. The man would carefully wind up and pitch an imaginary ball to an imaginary batter. After watching this imaginary pitching practice for half an hour every morning, the business man would then go on to work.

A friend who knew the businessman did this, asked him about it.

"Well," the businessman said, "If business keeps up like it has been for the past year, I'll probably be in there playing ball with him. And I'm studying his style so he won't be able to strike me out."

691.   A young man asked his girlfriend to marry him. Since she had security in mind as well as love, she told him she couldn't marry him until after he had saved $1,000. So, they continued to go together with no more mention of marriage.

A year later, she asked him how much he had saved.

"According to my last month's bank statement," he said, "I have $150 saved toward it."

"In that case," she said, "let's get married. I think that's close enough."

692.   A man and his wife had worked out a system to send dinner guests on their way at an early hour.

"Remember," the husband said, "if they are still here at 10:00 o'clock, you begin to tell them about the grandchildren; at 10:30, I'll tell them about my fishing trip; and if they haven't gone by 11:00, you begin to give them your political views."

POETRY

693.   A professor of poetry was trying to get his students to think creatively. When any of them would write an inspiring phrase or verse, he would talk about it in class and heap praise on them.

One day, one of his students turned in the title of a poem he was planning to write, "Walk with Light."

"What depth of thought," the professor said. "What a profound concept. Think how that wonderful thought can be developed—'walk with light.' Where did you get such a penetrating idea?"

"It's written on a sign underneath the stop light at the corner of First and Main Streets," the budding poet said.

POLITICAL

694.   Amendments to the Constitution ought not too frequently to be made . . . If continually tinkered with it will lose all its prestige and dignity, and the old instrument will be lost sight of altogether in a short time.

–Andrew Johnson

695.   Don't interfere with anything in the Constitution. That must be maintained, for it is the only safeguard of our liberties.

–Abraham Lincoln

696.   A government is not by the people when one party fastens its control upon the country and perpetuates its power by cajoling and betraying the people . . . instead of serving them.

–Grover Cleveland

697.   No party can be safely trusted with the interests of the people or the Government without it possesses a fixed, honest, and enlightened purpose.

–William McKinley

495, 497, 657.

POLITICIAN

698.   The candidate had been speaking for 40 minutes and was now winding up his speech. As he waved his arms for emphasis, he shouted, "We need reform. We need educational reform. We need housing reform. We need tax reform. We need . . ."

Before he could finish that sentence, a voice in the back shouted out, "Chloroform."

699. When an Arkansas candidate for public office announced at a big barbecue that he was 'a favorite son,' a voice was heard to say, "That's the most obvious unfinished sentence that was ever uttered in the State of Arkansas."

700. The ambitious young politician had delivered his most powerful campaign speech. When he had finished haranguing the crowd for 40 minutes, he said, "Now, are there any questions?"

"Yes," cried out one man in the crowd, "who else is running?"

476, 725.

POLITICS

701. The Congressman had spoken to the political science students at a large university and was in the midst of a question-and-answer period.

One student raised his hand and asked, "Sir, how do I get started in politics?"

"You're already started," the Congressman said, "every day you are in the university, you are spending somebody else's money."

666, 796.

POWER

702. See to the government. See that the government does not acquire too much power. Keep a check upon your rulers. Do this, and liberty is safe.

–William Henry Harrison

703.   I believe in power; but I believe that responsibility should go with power.

–Theodore Roosevelt

458, 625, 696.

PRACTICE

704.   The violin teacher said to her reluctant little pupil, "Look at it this way, Willy, the more you practice on the violin, the stronger your pitching arm will get."

PRAYER

705.   Church was over and two women had been chatting for some minutes in the parking lot. As they were telling each other goodbye, one woman realized that she did not have her purse. So, she rushed back into the church and to the pew where she had been sitting. The purse was not there.

As she stood there looking upset and bewildered, the minister approached with her purse in his hand. "I found this in the pew right after the church service," he said. "I thought I had better pick it up and take charge of it because someone in the congregation might see it and think it was an answer to his prayer."

458, 536, 719, 790.

PREACHER

706.   As I close my talk today, I want to say I hope I don't have the same kind of experience I did when I spoke recently in Lancaster County, Pennsylvania. That's where the Amish live. They have the Amish, the Dunkards and the Mennonites. After my speech, I had to take a bus back to the hotel in town and I sat in the back across from a Dunkard preacher. He had on his long black coat and that odd-looking hat that they wear. He had a beard that came almost to his waist. At the next corner, when the bus stopped, a drunk got on. He got into an argument with the bus driver. The driver finally quieted him down and sent him toward the back of the bus.

He staggered back to where we were and as he was holding on to the strap, he looked down at that preacher. "Well, look at you. All dressed up in that funny-looking uniform. And wearing a beard. What are you, a wrestler?"

The preacher jumped up and stood there in all of his dignity and said, "I'll have you know I'm a Dunkard pastor."

"Well, shake hands, friend, that's what the bus driver just called me."

710, 747.

PREPAREDNESS

707.   We shall more certainly preserve peace when it is well understood that we are prepared for war.

–Andrew Jackson

708.   There is nothing so likely to produce peace as to be well prepared to meet an enemy.

–George Washington

709.   America cannot be an ostrich with its head in the sand.

–Woodrow Wilson

658, 683, 684.

PRESTIGE

710.   It was a pleasure speaking to such a fine gathering tonight. You have been wonderful to me. I am proud to have been in your company. Right at this moment, I feel like the drunk who was staggering down the street late at night on his way home. His preacher happened to pass in his car, and he stopped and picked up the drunk and took him home. When they arrived in front of the drunk's house, the drunk said to the minister, "Thanks for the ride home. Now come up to the front door with me. When my wife opens the door, I want her to see who I was out with tonight."

PRETTY GIRL

711.   Now, I have come to that part of my speech that is the same as asking a pretty girl for a date. If she says she'll think it over—it already is.

717.

PRINCIPLES

712.   We should try to guide ourselves by general principles and not get lost in particulars.

—Calvin Coolidge

713.   Men and times change—but principles—never.

—Grover Cleveland

PROBLEMS

714.   From some of the things I have talked about today, you may think we have a lot of problems facing us. I thought of the troubles a friend of mine has. The other morning, before he could get out of his house and head for work, he had four long-distance calls. Everyone seemed to have a problem. And everybody wanted him to get on a plane that day and come help out. He finally told his wife to forget about his breakfast. He rushed out of the house as fast as he could go. Then, when he stepped into the garage he discovered his car wouldn't start. So he called a taxi to take him to work.

While he was waiting for the taxi, he got another call— this time from Chicago—about another problem. Finally, the taxi came and my friend rushed out, piled in the back seat and yelled. "All right, let's get going."

"Where do you want me to take you?" the taxi driver asked.

"I don't care where we go," the man shouted. "I've got problems everywhere."

662.

PROGRESS

715.   The office manager of a bank had been complaining to his wife about being overly tired at night and with having terrible pains in his back. Then, one day when he came home from work he said, "I've found out what's been causing my back trouble. As I told you, an interior decorator has just redesigned the office and furnished it with some of that ultramodern Scandinavian furniture. And I discovered today that for the past two weeks I have been sitting in my wastebasket."

716.   Never look back unless you are planning to go that way.

PROMISE

717.   A real estate agent was showing a woman an apartment which he was trying to rent. She looked like a movie star—sexy, beautiful. As he led her down the hall he said, "In this part of the apartment we have the master bedroom, a small sewing room, a bath, and den."

Instantly, she gave him a big smile and said, "And den what?"

PSYCHIATRIST

718.   Not long ago I was invited to speak at the state mental hospital to a group who were receiving psychiatric treatment. I had been talking for about two minutes when a man in the back stood up and shouted, "You're no psychiatrist. You don't know what you are talking about. Besides, you are talking too much. Shut up and sit down."

I stopped and said to the superintendent, "I'll wait a minute until you put that man out."

"Put him out?" the superintendent said. "Certainly not. That poor man has been here for eight years, and that's the first time he has ever said anything that makes any sense."

And the more I think about, maybe that fellow did make sense—and that's what I'm going to do. Thank you for listening to me.

PUNISHMENT

719.   A little girl had been sent to her room as punishment. After a while she reappeared in a happy mood.

"Well, Mamma," she said, "I've thought things over and I prayed."

"That's fine," said her mother. "Now that should help you be a good little girl."

"Oh, I didn't pray to be good," she said. "I asked God to help you put up with me."

QUICK THINKING

720.   The third-grade teacher made two of her pupils stay after school for talking in class. She told them that as punishment, they would have to write their names on the blackboard 500 times before they could go home. After half an hour, one of them stopped writing and complained to the teacher. "This isn't fair," he said. "She's through already because her name is May Sims, and I'll be here 'til dark because my name is George Horace Willingham."

721.   The TV director had advertised for a gag writer. "We are looking for a man who can think on his feet; who can ad lib; who can feed lines to our panelists fast, fast, fast. Have you ever had any experience along that line?"

"That's my specialty," the man said.

"Let's see you give me a fast one. Quick, one that fits this situation. Right now," the director shouted at him.

The gag writer jumped out of his chair, opened the door to the office and yelled down the hall to a roomful of waiting applicants, "Okay, all you guys. You can go home. The job's been filled."

RECOMMENDATION

722. When the speaker had finished his address at the big banquet and was shaking hands with people and receiving numerous compliments, he overheard a woman say to his wife, "Your husband is good. Does he get paid a lot for making speeches?"

"No," the speaker's wife said, "he's good for nothing. In fact, he's been good for nothing ever since I married him."

723. Thanks for listening to me. I spoke last week for 20 minutes and when I was finished everybody said they were satisfied.

RECORD

724. As her mother passed the little girl's room, she saw her lying in the middle of the floor on her stomach, singing happily. A few minutes later she came into the little girl's room and saw her lying on her back singing another song.

"Are you playing some sort of game?" her mother asked.

"Yes," the little girl said. "I'm an LP record and I just turned myself over. Now, I'm singing my other side."

REPUTATION

725. The Congressman was running for reelection. His opponent had been attacking him with a vicious smear campaign.

"I will not stoop to answer his filthy accusations," the Congressman said. "I never have campaigned on anybody's shortcomings. I've always been elected on my own."

726.   Speak with contempt of no man. Everyone hath a tender sense of reputation. And every man hath a sting, which he may, if provoked too far, dart out at one time or another.

–Robert Burton

727.   Associate yourself with men of good quality if you esteem your own reputation; for 'tis better to be alone than in bad company.

–George Washington

465, 736.

RESCUE

728.   The man was in the middle of the river, drowning. Suddenly, from the center span of the high bridge the hero came to the rescue. He hit the water with a mighty splash and within moments had begun to tread water and hold the drowning man's head out of water. Moments later a rescue boat picked both of them up and headed for shore.

Immediately, the hero was surrounded by well-wishers and members of the news media. "Congratulations," a TV reporter cried out. "You're a hero for jumping from the bridge to save this man's life. Do you have anything you'd like to say?"

"Yes," the hero said, "I'd like to know who pushed me."

RESPECT

729.   A farmer yelled at his son and said, "Bring me the axe."

But the boy just sat on the porch whittling and ignored his father.

A stranger, who was visiting the family, said, "Didn't you hear your father speak to you?"

"Oh, sure, I heared him," said the boy, "but I don't pay the man no mind. Neither does Maw or Sis, and between us we just about got the dog so he don't either."

RESPONSIBILITY

730.   Every man is the architect of his own fortune.

–Appius Claudius

703.

RESULTS

731.   There is no limit to the good you can do if you don't care who gets the credit.

424, 555.

RIGHT

732.   Let us have faith that right makes might, and in that faith let us to the end dare to do our duty as we understand it.

–Abraham Lincoln

733.   Right is right, even if everyone is against it; and wrong is wrong, even if everyone is for it.

–William Penn

734.   Don't take the wrong side of an argument just because your opponent has taken the right side.

–Baltasar Gracian

735.   Minorities often have been right, but they cease to be right when they use disorderly means.

–Woodrow Wilson

496.

RUMOR

736.   The speaker was surprised when he arrived at the civic club luncheon to find nobody there except the president, the secretary, the sergeant-at-arms and two members. The other 150 members were nowhere to be seen.

"Did you announce that I was going to address the meeting?" the speaker asked the president.

"No, we didn't," the president said, "but it sure looks as though the word leaked out doesn't it?"

564.

SAFETY

737.   A small boy was stretching as high as he could but the doorbell was just a few inches out of reach.

A stranger who was passing by felt sorry for the little fellow and picked him up and held him so he could ring the bell.

"Now, what?" the man said to the youngster.

"I don't know about you," the kid said, "but I'm going to start running as fast as I can."

808.

SALESMANSHIP

738.   The young man who was selling cemetery property called at the home of a senior citizen. When the lady of the house came to the door, he introduced himself and began to talk to her about the wisdom of buying a cemetery lot as a hedge against rising prices. She interrupted his sales presentation to explain that she and her husband already owned a plot in another cemetery.

For a moment the young man seemed to be at a loss for words. Then he said, "That's nice. I hope you will be happy there."

739.   A young fellow about 12 years old went into the bank to deposit $75 in his savings account. The banker, being friendly and interested in the boy, said, "That's a pretty big deposit. How did you earn the money?"

"Selling Christmas cards," the little boy said.

"You did real well," the banker said. "You must have sold cards to a lot of people in your neighborhood."

"No, sir," the boy said. "One family bought all of them. Their dog bit me."

740.   A new vacuum cleaner salesman was looking downcast.

"Come, come!" said his boss. "Don't look so down-in-the mouth. It's not easy at first, but you'll soon catch on. With a little experience you'll do all right."

"Oh, it isn't that," said the salesman. "When I got home last night, I practiced my sales talk on my wife, and now I've got to buy her a vacuum cleaner."

547, 770.

SCHOOL

741.   The pretty little college girl who wasn't doing too well in her history class stopped by the professor's office a couple of weeks before the final examination.

With a "come-hither" smile and a seductive tone in her voice she said, "I've just got to get a good grade on the final examination, professor. I'd do anything—anything, you understand—to get a passing grade."

"Do you mean you will do anything I ask you, just to pass the test?" he said with eagerness in his voice.

"Yes," she replied demurely.

"Then go home and study," he said, "and you'll make it."

436, 516.

SECRETARY

742.   The president of a paper manufacturing company hired a new secretary because of her beauty and not because of her typing ability. He figured anybody could handle the small amount of correspondence that he took care of personally. For example, on her first day as his secretary he dictated only one letter. It went to a publisher. As he finished dictating he said to her. "You can get the address of the company off of their letterhead."

He discovered his mistake the next day when the letter was returned from the post office marked insufficient address.

The envelope read, "Prentice-Hall, Inc., Tokyo, London, Sydney, Toronto, New Delhi, Singapore, Englewood Cliffs."

638.

SELF

743.   Oh, wad some power the gifte gie us
To see oursels as others see us!
It wad frae mony a blunder free us,
And foolish notion.

–Robert Burns
"To a Louse"

SENIOR CITIZENS

744.   An elderly fellow who had trouble remembering important dates was leaving his house to go to town when his wife kissed him goodbye and said, "Don't you remember what day this is?"

He didn't remember whether it was her birthday or wedding anniversary or some other important date. So, he stopped by the drug store and had a two-pound box of candy sent over to the house. Then, when he had run his errands and headed home, he stopped in a shopping center and bought her a bottle of perfume and had it gift-wrapped.

When he came home and walked in the front door, he said, "Surprise, honey, look what I brought you to help celebrate this wonderful day."

She rushed into his arms and hugged him and kissed him and said, "My, how nice. This is the happiest Ground-Hog Day I can ever remember."

745.   Let us cherish and love old age; for it is full of pleasure, if one knows how to use it. The best morsel is reserved to the last.

–Seneca

SKELETONS

746.   Two skeletons that were used in a university class in anatomy had been put in storage. They had been hanging in a closet for several weeks when one of them said to the other, "What are we doing shut up in this closet, anyway?"

The other skeleton said, "I don't know for sure. But, if we had any guts, we'd get out of here."

SPEAKER

747.   The visiting preacher had been invited to the big noon "dinner-on-the-ground" before he was to preach the afternoon service at an all-day meeting at the rural church.

One of the ladies of the church offered to fill his plate for him but he stopped her. "I never eat," he said, "before I preach. I find that it keeps me from preaching a good sermon."

After the service was over, a friend asked that same lady what she thought of the sermon. "As far as I am concerned," she said, "he might as well of et."

748.   The speaker had been giving a long-winded and boring talk about his travels out West. After an hour, he launched into a description of the Grand Canyon. "There I stood," he said, "standing on the rim of one of the natural wonders of the world. I was overcome with awe as I gazed into that huge abyss yawning before me."

A voice in the back called out, "Tell us. Was it yawning before you arrived on the scene?"

749.   A man tiptoed out of the banquet room during the middle of the main speech. As he stepped onto the front steps of the hotel to get a breath of fresh air, he met another man who had left the banquet before him.

"Has the speaker finished what he had to say yet?" the first man asked.

"Oh, he finished that five minutes after he started," the second man said, "but he's still talking."

750.   A young actor was telling his father about his first part in an off-Broadway play. "It's going to be great," he said to his father, "I play the part of a man who has been married for 26 years."

"You've made a good start in show business, son," his father said. "Do a good job in that role and one of these days you'll get a speaking part."

751.   Once there was a little baby cabbage who said to his mother, "Mommy, I'm worried about something. As I sit in this row of cabbages and grow and grow and grow day after day, how will I know when to stop growing?"

"The rule to follow," the mamma cabbage said, "Is to quit when you are a head."

752.   One time a man shot an after-dinner speaker who talked too long and didn't say anything of interest.

Immediately the man turned himself in to the sheriff, and said, "I just shot an after-dinner speaker."

"You are in the wrong place," the sheriff said. "You should go to the game warden's office. You collect the bounty there."

753.   When her husband returned home in the evening after making a speech at a civic club, his wife said, "Well, how did it go? Did they like your speech?"

"They certainly did," her husband said. "When I finished and sat down, everybody said it was the best thing I'd ever done."

754.   "Do you know what it is to go before an audience," a man asked his friend.

"No," said his friend. "Every time I make a speech, the audience goes before I do."

755.   Two things are improved by shortening. They are biscuits and speeches.

429, 459, 472, 477, 478, 492, 593, 609, 664, 665, 722, 723, 774, 781, 787.

SPLIT

756. The stockbroker called one of his clients, a recent widow who had only recently made her first stock purchase—50 shares of Procter & Gamble. "I have some good news," he said. "We got word that Procter and Gamble is going to split."

"Oh, how terrible," she said. "They've been together for so many years."

STOP LIGHT

757. A woman driver came to a stop light when the light was red and stopped as she should. But her car stalled, and she couldn't get it started. While she was pushing on the starter the light turned to green, then amber, then back to red. At that time, a man in a car behind her honked his horn and shouted, "What are you waiting for, lady, your favorite color?"

STRENGTH

758.
 A good cause makes a stout heart and a strong arm.

–Thomas Fuller

458, 521, 567, 797.

SUCCESS

759. The Little Leaguer put all he had into his swing. He hit a line drive directly to the pitcher who was so surprised that he tried to catch it with his bare hand. But he dropped the ball. In his excitement over his error, he threw the ball about two feet out of reach of the first baseman, and the batter headed for second base. The same thing happened at second. The second baseman fumbled the ball and it rolled toward left field where the shortstop and the left fielder ran into each other as they both tried to pick it up. Finally, the center fielder recovered it and threw it toward home. It got to the catcher about two seconds after the runner had scored.

Later when his teammates were congratulating the batter, he said, "I feel great. That's the first home run I ever hit."

760. A minister's wife was suffering with a bad cold and stayed home one Sunday morning instead of going to church. When the minister came home, his wife asked him about the morning service. "What did you preach about this morning?"

"I talked about charity," he said. "I told them that it was a duty of the rich to give to the poor."

"How did it go over?" his wife asked.

"About 50-50," the minister said. "I convinced the poor."

761. No man knows what he can do till he tries.

–Publilius Syrus

762. The secret of success is constancy to purpose.

–Benjamin Disraeli

440, 474, 567, 617, 739, 810, 811.

SURPRISE

763. The wealthy man had moved to Florida from Michigan when he retired. When he was in the hospital with only a few days to live, his family was faced with a delicate question to ask him. "Before we moved down here," his wife said, "you bought cemetery property for us in Michigan. Then, not long ago you bought two plots down here. I hate to ask you such a question at a time like this, but where do you wish to be buried?"

He looked at her with a twinkle in his eye and said, "Why don't you surprise me?"

SYMPATHY

764. A recent widow was being visited by a lady from the church who was trying hard to be sympathetic.

"I suppose your husband left you quite a lot?" she asked.

"Yes, he did," the widow said, "nearly every time he got a chance."

TALENT

765.   Let every man practice the art that he knows best.

–Cicero

579.

TEACHER

766.   A mother was upset over her little girl's report card and called her teacher at school. "Isn't she trying?" she asked the teacher.

The teacher sighed and said, "She certainly is."

470, 582, 589.

TEACHING

767.   They who educate children well, are more to be honored than they who produce them; for these only gave them life, those the art of living well.

–Aristotle

768.   What nobler employment, or more valuable to the state, than that of the man who instructs the rising generation?

–Cicero

517.

TELEPHONE

769.   The man's teenage daughter answered the phone. Then, to his surprise, after half an hour she hung up.

"Hey," he said, "that was a short conversation for you. You usually talk for an hour. What's the matter?"

"Nothing's the matter," she said. "That time it was a wrong number."

614.

TELEVISION

770.   As the opera singer was into her third number on a much publicized "television special," a woman said to her husband, "Isn't she wonderful? I hear that her singing has been responsible for the sale of thousands and thousands of television sets."

"I can understand that," her husband. "After listening to her for another five minutes, I'll be ready to sell this one."

TENACITY

771.   Our greatest glory is not in never falling but in rising every time we fall.

—Confucius

TEXAS

772.   A Texan was having a heart-to-heart talk with his little boy. "Son," the father said, "I just heard you ask that man if he was from Texas. You must never do that. If he is from Texas, he'll tell you. And if he isn't from Texas, you shouldn't embarrass him."

THANKS

773   A second-grade teacher had given her students the project of making their own personal Christmas cards for their parents. Instead of having them struggle over individual messages, she suggested that the kids look through cards that had already come in the mail and copy something that seemed suitable.

One little boy copied the message from a card received by his father from the local hardware store. His card read, "It has been a pleasure doing business with you."

774. A speaker once thanked his audience by saying, "A polite person is one who listens with interest to things he knows all about, when they are told to him by someone who knows little or nothing about them. Thank you for being so polite to me this evening."

545, 681, 711.

THEATRE

775. A woman was attending the theatre for the first time. When the first act was over, she started to leave. "I certainly did enjoy the play," she said to the head usher as she walked through the lobby.

"Aren't you going to stay for the rest of play?" he asked.

She smiled at him warmly as she said, "I don't see any point in doing that. Because it says right here in the program, Act II, same as Act I."

TIMING

776. One Sunday, during the church service, the wife of a deacon became worried about the roast at home in the oven. She thought she had left the oven on. Worried, she sent a note to her husband by one of the ushers. The usher misunderstood her and thought the note was for the preacher. He tiptoed down the aisle and laid it on the pulpit.

The preacher paused in his sermon, opened the note, and read, "Please go home and turn off the gas."

777. The young man was proposing to his girlfriend. Full of romance because of the great moment, he began like this: "Darling, please marry me. If you do, my life will be filled with sunshine. The dark clouds will roll away and the blue skies, dotted with billowy clouds will . . ."

Right there she interrupted him by saying, "Harry, you're talking too much. How about putting that ring on my finger and forget the weather report?"

778. An industrial consultant was making a study of the working habits of the men in a manufacturing plant. Speaking to one of the foremen, he asked, "Do the men in your department drop their tools the moment the quitting whistle blows?"

"Some of them do," the foreman said, "but the neat and orderly ones always have theirs put away and locked up by that time."

779. Suddenly, in the middle of his lunch, a man looked at the clock on the wall and made a rush for his hat and coat.

"It's two o'clock," he said to the man he was having lunch with. "I've got to get over to the corner. My wife is supposed to meet me there at one o'clock, and I don't dare be late."

780. A minister was being entertained at dinner and the other guests were praising his sermon. One of them turned to his host's young son, who was at the table, and asked, "Young man, what did you think of the sermon?"

"Oh, it was all right," he said, "except he passed up three real good places where he could have stopped."

781. It had started to rain during the meeting, so the speaker felt he should cut his talk short. "And now," he said, "I shall conclude my talk for this evening. In fact, I'm afraid I've already kept you too long."

"Oh, keep right on," said a voice from the rear. "It's still raining and most of us didn't bring umbrellas."

782. The bell rang in the museum to announce ten minutes to closing time. As the museum's guards herded the people to the exit doors, one of them said, "I've worked here for 15 years, and it's always the same. There's always somebody who is the last one to leave."

783. A kindergarten teacher was standing in front of a class of 5-year-olds during their exercise period. As she waved her arms and tapped out the rhythm with her foot, she kept saying, "Hurry up and wear yourselves out—wear yourselves out. Hurry up and wear yourselves out."

784. For five years, the stockroom man had been coming to work late. Finally, the boss called him in and said, "Look, Joe, instead of waiting until you have worked for us 25 years to give you a wrist watch, we are giving you this alarm clock—now!"

785. As I come to the close of my speech, I feel exactly as I did two weeks ago. I had the most amazing dream. I dreamed I was speaking to an audience exactly like this one. And when I woke up—I WAS.

786. The preacher had been talking for more than an hour. Finally, when he seemed to pause for breath, he said, "My friends, what more can I say?"

From the back of the church a weary-sounding voice said, "Amen."

787. The speaker was chatting with a friend. "How did your speech go last night?" his friend asked.

"I made a great hit," the speaker said.

"What did you talk about?" his friend asked.

"About five minutes," the speaker said.

788. A budding young musician asked the great orchestra leader, "What do you have to know in order to play the cymbals in an orchestra?"

"Nothing, really," the orchestra leader said, "except *when*."

789. The visitor at the jail asked the man in the cell, "And why are you locked up?"

"I suppose they think I'd go home if I wasn't," he said.

503, 506, 536, 723, 751, 764.

TOWN CRIER

790.   List, good people all!
Past ten o'clock the hour I call.
Now say your prayers and take your rest,
With conscience clear and sins confessed.
I bid you all good night! Good night!

TRAVEL

791.   A man was standing in front of the country store when his friend drove up in a fancy motor home. "Hi, Joe." the first man said, "It looks like you're getting ready to take a trip."

"That's right," his friend said. "My wife and I are repairing to take off for a two-week vacation out West. Grand Canyon and all those places."

"You said you were 'repairing' to leave," the first man said. "You really meant to say 'preparing.' 'Repairing,' means 'fixing.' "

"That's what I said," his friend replied, "my wife and I are fixing to take a trip out West."

561.

TRUTH

792.   A man was behind in his rent and his landlord was trying to collect it.

"I'm sorry," the man told the landlord, "I'm out of work and I can't pay you anything this week."

"I'm tired of hearing your excuses," the landlord said. "That's what you said last week and the week before and the week before that."

"Well," the man said, "you'll have to agree that I have kept my word."

793.   "I wish there were some easy way to get rid of that girlfriend of mine," a young fellow said to his friend.

"Why don't you just tell her to get going?" his friend

asked. "Are you afraid she will go around telling lies about you?"

"No," the young fellow said, "I'm afraid she'll go around telling the truth.'

794.   I have faith in the people . . . The danger is, in their being misled.Let them know the truth, and the country is safe.

–Abraham Lincoln

427.

UNDERSTANDING

795.   The minister was starting a new Sunday school class. "We are going to study the Bible in great depth," he said, "because I am sure there is much of it that we don't understand. And I am sure that you feel that is important or you wouldn't be in the class."

"Not exactly," one of the older men said, "I never worry much about the part I don't understand. It's the part that I do understand that bothers me."

477, 478, 582.

UNITY

796.   The visiting Congressman was discussing local politics with one of the voters. "Why in the world is there so much fighting within the party around here? Can't the Democrats in this town get together?"

"Get together?" the voter said, "Why, in this town it takes the sheriff and three of his deputies to keep them apart."

797.   All your strength is in your union.
            All your danger is in discord;
            Therefore be at peace henceforward,
            And as brothers live together.

–Henry Wadsworth Longfellow

VOCATION

798.   The vocation of every man and woman is to serve other people.

–Leo Tolstoy

WAIT

799.   The man with the toothache had been waiting his turn in the dentist's waiting room for more than an hour. Finally, the nurse escorted him into the dentist's inner office.

"I'm sorry you had to wait so long," the dentist said, "but the gentleman ahead of you had a serious abscess that took more time than I figured it would."

"Oh, that's all right," the man said, "but did you know that there are 32,661 stars in the beautiful blue wallpaper in your waiting room?"

800.   The doctor's waiting room was crowded. And as often is the case, several patients had been waiting as much as an hour or more beyond their appointed time. Finally, an elderly man stood up and said in a voice that everyone could hear, "I've waited long enough. I guess I'll just have to go back home and die a natural death."

801.   A young man was calling on his girlfriend. When he rang the doorbell, the girl's father came to the door. "Come in," he said. "Betty says she will be ready right away. Would you care for a game of chess while you are waiting?"

WANDERLUST

802.   An old fellow had lived in the same house in a small southern town for 40 years. Then one day, he suddenly sold his place and moved into the house across the street. "What did you move for," a friend asked him.

"Oh," he said, "I suppose it's just my natural wanderlust coming out."

WEATHER

803.   I think I have covered just about everything in my speech except the weather, so before I sit down I would like to say a word about that.

Back home on the farm, one time when I was a boy, we had a blizzard. Of course, when we had that kind of weather, the schools would shut down. So they closed the schools for three days. Then, on the first day that school was open, the teacher noticed a little fellow on the front row with his head on his desk, sound asleep. She woke him up and said, "What's the matter? Why are you sleeping in school? Are you sick?"

The little boy said, "No, I'm not sick. I just didn't get any sleep last night. It was the chicken thieves. You know, they've been stealing our chickens for a long time and Pa said the next time they came around he was going to get himself a couple of dead chicken thieves. And last night in the middle of the night he heard 'em. So Pa jumped out of bed and ran for the chicken house. He didn't even take time to put on his trousers. He ran out in his nightshirt. He grabbed his shotgun by the back door and loaded both barrels. He put his fingers on both triggers and he tiptoed out through all that snow to the chicken house. He heard 'em inside and he was easing that door open real careful-like with his gun pointed inside. Well, you know that old dog of ours named Towser? He came up behind Pa with his cold nose. And we were up all night long last night picking and cleaning chickens."

WIFE

804.   A drunk staggered into a small neighborhood cocktail lounge and shouted. "Happy New Year, everybody."

The bartender said to him, "Friend, for your information, this is not the New Year. This happens to be the first of April."

"You mean it's April already?" the drunk asked. "Brother, my wife will kill me for staying on a bender this long."

805. "Dad," asked a young fellow who was studying his homework, "What is a counterirritant?"

"A counterirritant?" said his father, who was the manager of a supermarket, "is a woman who stands in front of the meat counter and inspects every package of meat there before she buys a can of tuna fish."

422, 444, 503, 534, 750, 779.

WISDOM

806. A man should never be ashamed to own he has been in the wrong, which is but saying, in other words, that he is wiser today than he was yesterday.

–Alexander Pope

807. The cat, having sat upon a hot stove lid, will not sit upon a hot stove lid again. Nor upon a cold stove lid.

–Mark Twain

808. It is best not to swap horses while crossing the river.

–Abraham Lincoln

502, 582.

WORK

809. Perhaps the most valuable result of all education is the ability to make yourself do the things you have to do, when it ought to be done, whether you like it or not. It is the first lesson that ought to be learned.

–Thomas H. Huxley

810. Work is not a curse, it is the prerogative of intelligence, the only means to manhood, and the measure of civilization. Savages do not work.

–Calvin Coolidge

811.   The law of worthy work well done is the law of successful American life.

–Theodore Roosevelt

567, 778.

Thematic Index for Closers

The numbers refer to the Closers in Chapter 5